ABOUT THE

Jim Pym became a Buddhist in the early twenties, and encountered the Society of Friends a few years later. After working in a number of different fields, including several years as a professional musician, he became a bookseller, and eventually manager of the Friends Book Centre in London for 13 years. He then moved into publishing as Literature Secretary for Quaker Home Service. In 1995, he was invited to become the Clerk of Quakers Uniting in Publications, an international organisation of Friends involved in all aspects of Quaker literature.

His interest in Buddhism remained in parallel with his membership of the Quakers, and he is currently on the Council of the Buddhist Society in London, and editor of a journal, Pure Land Notes. He was one of the founders of the Friends Interfaith Group, and is a member of the Friends Fellowship of Healing, having been involved in spiritual healing work for many years. He has led many retreats and study weekends for Quakers and others, and has written widely on healing, meditation, Buddhism and Quaker concerns.

LISTENING TO THE LIGHT

HOW TO BRING QUAKER SIMPLICITY AND INTEGRITY INTO OUR LIVES

Jim Pym

RIDER

LONDON • SYDNEY • AUCKLAND • JOHANNESBURG

3 5 7 9 10 8 6 4 2

First published in 1999 by Rider,
an imprint of Ebury Press, Random House,
20 Vauxhall Bridge Road, London SW1V 2SA
www.randomhouse.co.uk

Random House Australia (Pty) Limited
20 Alfred Street, Milsons Point, Sydney,
New South Wales 2061, Australia

Random House New Zealand Limited
18 Poland Road, Glenfield,
Auckland 10, New Zealand

Random House South Africa (Pty) Limited
Endulini, 5A Jubilee Road,
Parktown 2193, South Africa

The Random House Group Limited Reg. No. 954009

Papers used by Rider are natural, recyclable products made
from wood grown in sustainable forests.

Printed by Creative Print and Design (Wales)

A CIP catalogue record for this book
is available from the British Library

ISBN 0-7126-7020-3

CONTENTS

To Beryl

PREFACE

In my journey along the Quaker Way I have met many wonderful people. Being human, they have had to face all the usual difficulties of living in this world. Yet they have an inner peace which not only helps them, but is also able to inspire and comfort others. Some have experienced extra difficulties, which at first sight might seem to be self-inflicted, but were actually the result of following their own Light, and affirming their deeply held beliefs when they were in conflict with the way of the world. They have also attained a great inner peace and joy. This is the other side of the coin of conscience.

I am profoundly grateful for all the input that they have made to my life, and to this book. Without them it could never have been written. Following the Quaker Way has been for me a mixture of joys and sorrows, and while I have never had to put my life on the line for my beliefs – as some people have had to do – I have certainly had to put my faith there. Writing this book has been fun, but it has also made me re-assess what I have discovered in more than thirty years' association with Friends.

A Friend – in both senses – who read the first draft of the manuscript, pointed out that there are three strands to it. When I re-read it I could see that this was so. The first is personal, even autobiographical in places. This is because I could not write about something that has been so much a part of my spiritual life in any other way. I take full responsibility for all I have to say, even though I know that there will be Friends who disagree with me. But that is the nature of Quakers today. I hope we can still remain F/friends.

I have to write in this manner because of the way I came to Quakers. Many – I might almost say most – Friends today have come to the Society as refugees from other churches. I came to the Society as a Buddhist, not to escape from Buddhism, but because I thought that the Quaker meeting was a meditation group. While I soon learned that it is not – at least, not in the Buddhist sense – I did discover that there was much more to Quakerism than I had supposed. So I stayed. I did not, and still do not, find any conflict between Buddhism and Quakerism, but there are Friends who do. I was a Buddhist when I joined the Society, and have remained one ever since. However I am not a Buddhist/Quaker or a Quaker/Buddhist. I do not think there is any such thing. I am a Buddhist *and* a Quaker. I feel that probably makes me both a Buddhist and a Christian; or possibly neither. Labels are not important – unless you want them to be.

I certainly have learned to appreciate the life and teachings of Jesus as I have grown older and I thank both Buddhism and Quakerism for that. My experience in Buddhism has led me to see them in a way that I think is close to that of early Quakers, and this might not have been possible had I just stayed within the Christian religion. I am perfectly clear that the Christian roots of Quakerism are an essential part of its very existence, and something that I would not want to deny. They are an essential which Quakers must not ignore if they wish to maintain their identity.

The second strand is that it is a book *about* Quakerism, and *about* Quakers and all that has inspired them over the past three hundred years. It is primarily about what I see as the essence of Quakerism; deep inner listening to the still small voice of the Spirit of God within each person. I believe that this message has a great deal to give to our world today. It is not – except where necessary – a book about the Society of Friends, or about any of the other Quaker organisations throughout the world. I deeply believe that what Quakers have discovered is more important than any organisation. While the Society today has much to give, organisations by their very nature tend to stifle the free flow of the Spirit which is, to me, the essence of Quakerism. But then I suppose I am that strange mixture of a spiritual anarchist and a traditionalist.

Some of my readers may be looking for a spiritual home. They may, after reading this book, go to their local meeting. If they find what they are looking for, they may wish to become members. All this is up to the individual, or rather, up to the Divine Light that guides each of us. I have read that Voltaire said that saving people is Divine business, and we should leave it to God. Whether he did or not, this is a sentiment I agree with. Quakerism is about being guided by that element of God within us, and it does not really matter what name we give it. It is freedom and discipline, and the tension between these two is what makes it interesting. So feel free to read, and may you find what you seek – somewhere.

The third strand in the book is that it is, to some extent, a 'how to' book. It suggests ways in which you may, if you feel inspired to, incorporate ideas into your own life. Because I believe the Quaker message has something to give to the world – and that means people – I have made suggestions, particularly in the last chapter. It is entirely up to you when, if and how you use the ideas I am sharing with you. Even if you never go near a Quaker meeting there may be ideas and practices which will be helpful to you on your journey. I must add here that I believe that if you do not experience a Quaker meeting for worship at least once – and, because no two are the same, preferably several times – you may miss some of its subtleties. And you may miss a valuable experience. But that is up to you. Quakers do not proselytise, and I certainly have no intention of doing so on their behalf.

Finally, there are a number of conventions that I have adopted which might need some explanation. The word 'Friend' capitalised throughout the rest of the book indicates Quakers. On the rare occasions where I have used F/friend I am talking about people who are both Quakers and personal friends. I hope the text makes it clear.

Other words are capitalised where they are synonyms for God, for Quaker tradition uses a number of synonyms for God. To these, I have added one or two of my own. In one place, the word 'Friend' is used for God, but this is clear in the text. Where I am talking in traditionally Christian terms, I have used 'He' for God, but in other places I have used 'It'. There did not seem to be a place where 'She' was appropriate, so I have not used it, but I would have no difficulty in doing so. For me – and many others – God is both feminine and masculine, both and neither.

I have tried wherever possible to avoid the use of the masculine pronoun when referring to people in general. This use of inclusive language is a particular concern of Quakers today, and I have tried to honour it. However, occasionally, where this has not been possible, and I have had to use one or the other, I have usually used 'he'. I have also kept 'he' or 'man' where it is part of an original quote.

Quotations from a little booklet called *Advices and Queries* appear throughout the book, and the full text is found in Appendix 1. I do believe that this short work, published by the Society of Friends, is vital in understanding Quakers today, even if the language seems a little dated. A superscript number in brackets after each quotation indicates the section from which it has come. Superscript numbers without brackets indicate quotations from other sources, details of which can be found in the Notes and References section at the back of the book. Full references can be found in the Bibliography.

ACKNOWLEDGEMENTS

Thanks are especially due to David Goddard, who was in the first place largely responsible for suggesting that I might write the book, and has encouraged me throughout. There are many others with whom I worked at Friends House, notably Beth Allen, Clifford Barnard, Graham Garner, Harvey Gillman, Jim Holmes, Ian Kiek, John Punshon and Elisabeth Salisbury, all of whom gave encouragement in different ways. John Noble's sense of humour and ability to listen kept many of us going through difficult times. Malcolm Thomas, the Librarian at Friends House, read the manuscript and made many helpful suggestions.

My next-door neighbours, Cathy and Jonathan Stebbings, writers in their own right, read the manuscript at various times, and helped when I got stuck, in ways they may never know.

The members of Burford Meeting in Oxfordshire have, in various ways, but mostly through the depth of their worship, restored my faith in Quakerism at the time when it was very threatened. I will always be grateful to them. I would particularly like to thank Irene Glaister, who read the manuscript, and Roger Warner, who has been very patient with me when I should have been doing other things.

In the USA, the friendship of Liz Yeats of Friends General Conference, who is my co-clerk on Quakers Uniting in Publications, was always encouraging. Judith Randall, Quaker, Zen Buddhist, bird-watcher and friend, helped me through difficult times, often without knowing it.

The Joseph Rowntree Charitable Trust gave me a grant to record the memories of Quakers between the wars, and the changes in meetings that occurred up until the 1950s. From this experience I gained many insights into Quakerism that I did not have before, and which are incorporated into this book. They were also very understanding when I needed to temporarily suspend the project to write this book.

Judith Kendra, Editorial Director at Rider Books, came up with the original idea, and has been immensely supportive throughout.

My wife, Beryl, has always been there for me when life has been difficult, and when my faith has disappeared. We have also shared the spiritual search, and many good times. I have dedicated the book to her, and cannot say enough in gratitude.

Finally, there must be many F/friends whom I have omitted to mention, whose ideas and inspiration have been incorporated to a greater or lesser extent in this book. Space – and my bad memory – does not allow me to include you all, but please know that I am grateful and appreciate your lives and friendship.

I am grateful to Dr Rachel Pinney who, when she was alive, gave me permission to quote from her booklet,

Acknowledgements

Creative Listening. She was keen that as many people as possible should have the opportunity to practise the method that she pioneered. Thanks are also due to Joanne and Larry Spears, who waived copyright on their booklet, *Friendly Bible Study*, so that Friends could freely use their discoveries.

I am also grateful to Britain Yearly Meeting of the Religious Society of Friends for allowing me to quote from *Quaker Faith and Practice*, in particular the *Advices and Queries*, and to print the whole of the text of the *Advices* as an appendix. Thanks are also due to Quaker Home Service for permission to quote from a number of their publications.

Introduction

… these things we do not lay upon you as a rule or form to walk by, but that all, walking and abiding, these may be fulfilled in the Spirit, not from the letter, for the letter killeth, but the Spirit giveth life. (From the postscript to an epistle to 'the brethren in the north' issued by a meeting of the elders at Balby, 1656)

For nearly three hundred and fifty years there have been people who literally 'listen to the Light', and allow the fruits of their practice to govern their everyday lives. They are not members of some esoteric order, nor followers of some Eastern faith. In Britain, they are members of The Yearly Meeting of the Religious Society of Friends (Quakers) in Britain. In the USA, they are divided into a number of other groups called yearly meetings. I just call them all 'Friends' or 'Quakers'.

Their practice – and its fruits – has been an inspiration to me for more than twenty-five years. It is available to anyone who chooses to follow it, not as a rule, but as a guide to listening to – and following – their own Light. This Light is the Divine within each person, and within the whole of creation.

———◆———

Take heed, dear Friends, to the promptings of love and truth in your hearts. Trust them as the leadings of God whose Light shows us our darkness and brings us to new life. [1]

This book is an attempt to show what Quakers have learned and experienced over the years, and how the very best of this knowledge can be infused into the lives of anyone, whether or not they are religious in the normal sense of the word. Because Quakerism is above all a religion of experience, there has to be something of my own journey in the telling. I must tell it as I have found it, not only in order for it to make sense, but for me to be true to myself and my Friends. I cannot claim to speak for The Religious Society of Friends as a whole. No-one can. There *are* things that all Quakers hold in common, but since everything is subject to the inner revelation of the Spirit, it may be interpreted or expressed in many different ways.

All of the ideas that have come out of the Quaker experience are applicable to anyone who takes them seriously. They are the fruits of a practical mysticism for ordinary people. You will find them helpful (though not always comfortable) in your daily lives, and discover that they work. This is the most important thing, for Quakerism is above all a religion of everyday life. We do not see any separation between the spiritual and the secular. Or rather, the spiritual and the secular blend together in a way that makes it impossible to separate one from the other. When we remember – and that is the key factor – the spiritual permeates our daily lives.

The right religious attitude, as Quakers see it, allows the sacraments of other churches and the rituals of other faiths to be found in ordinary actions. Thus, *all* meals can be experienced as holy. In other traditions the sacred meal is called the Eucharist or *Prasad*. For Quakers, all nourishment, physical, mental and spiritual, is a gift from God for which we can give thanks. Similarly, all washing or bathing may be seen as baptism or a rite of purification. And all gathering in silence with the intention of seeking the experience of the Divine Presence is worship.

———◆———

Treasure your experience of God, however it
comes to you [2]

I became a Quaker by accident. At least, for many years I thought it was an accident. However the more I discover about the role of the Light in guiding a person's life, even if they are not aware of it, the more I wonder. Certainly, looking back, I can see a pattern which I was not aware of at the time. So now I am not so sure.

I was born and brought up in the Roman Catholic Church, and it was thought by all concerned – including myself – that I was going to be a priest. In time I asked too many questions, and eventually I left that church. I will of this everyone has direct access to God. They have no priests or ministers. Quakers meet in silence, not for meditation of a personal kind, but because they feel that this is the best way to discover the presence of God. In the silence, Quakers say, God's voice can be heard. From this they draw the power of the great paradox. They develop an inner peace and tranquillity, and at the same time a compassionate restlessness towards the suffering of the world. They also share with the Buddhists a belief in peace and non-violence.

Be honest with yourself. What unpalatable truths might you be evading? [11]

What have I personally learned in my association with Friends over the years? It has taught me that there *is* something of God within each person, even those in whom it seems impossible to find it. In fact, this Divine Presence is in all creation. I cannot claim that I always remember that it is so – in fact, I forget more often than I remember. But when I do remember it changes my life, and the world around me. These changes are usually not dramatic, but subtle, and at its best this has enabled me to ' … know an inward stillness, even amid the activities of daily life.'[3]

This Divine Presence takes many forms. Some *see* it as the Inward Light. Others *hear* it as the Still Small Voice. Whether you see or hear depends upon your temperament. Within the practice of yoga, it is recognised that there are different types of human beings. Some are devotional, others are more intellectual,

21

while a third group is more practical. There are different types of spiritual practice for each type. I have observed this among Friends, but the Quaker way of worship in the silence eventually transcends these differences and brings us to Oneness. The Inward Light and the Still Small Voice are One, and in the end it is the Oneness that really matters.

I have discovered that we can all contact the Spirit within us. We do not need the external aid of special ministers or special rituals. Through this Spirit, ordinary people have the potential to become extraordinary. Through It, I have come to realise that ordinary people *are* extraordinary. Because, in the words of Tennyson, this Spirit is 'Closer ... than breathing, nearer than hands and feet.'[1] It is there whether we acknowledge it or not, but when we do recognise it, and in the silence provide a space for it to act within our consciousness, It can transform our lives, and the lives of all around us.

In the preceding paragraphs I have referred to the Divine as 'It', but the Christian teaching, on which Quakerism is based, teaches us that God is personal, and can be experienced as a loving and forgiving Presence. It can be experienced as male or female, though for most Friends it equates with the presence of God or Christ. (Mother Julian of Norwich said that Christ is also our Mother, and some Quakers would confirm that experience.) I have come to know this Divine Power through the deep silence of the gathered group in Quaker worship, and discovered that the power of the group is greater than the sum of the individuals present. I have also found it through meditation. And I have learned that if I make the intention – even if I often fail to live up to it – to live my life as if it is so, then I can experience that Presence and Power in a very real way at any time. All this, for me, has been a powerful and life-changing message.

———◆———

Quakers are often thought of as being a withdrawn or closed group of people. Some even think that we have died out. We haven't. We are still here, and still leavening the world around us. (Another Quaker metaphor for the Divine within people is 'The Leaven'.) The spiritual search which gave rise to Quakerism has been a source of inspiration and a fountain of ideas for living for over three hundred years. It still is. That search began with looking for the reality of God in a world where religion was closely allied with worldly power, and rigidly controlled by narrow interpretations of Scripture. Questioning could lead to imprisonment and worse.

Quakerism is a part of the European Christian mystical tradition which combines spirituality with the practical life, and its particular insights give it a universal appeal which is particularly relevant to today's world. As a specific movement it started around the mid-seventeenth century. It arose out of the searching by many people for a religious voice that was true to the Holy Spirit. George Fox is often quoted as its 'founder', and while his teaching was vital to its formation as a movement, there were many others whose contribution was equally valuable. It was truly a movement of the Spirit. The famous Quaker historian, Rufus Jones, has shown that Quakerism was a part of the stream of mysticism which started with Dionysius and included Jacob Boehme, St

Francis of Assisi, Meister Eckhart and The Friends of God. There may or may not have been physical contact with these ideas, but the essence of their teachings and practices was in the air. When George Fox had his own personal revelation, and met up with others who were similarly searching, another link in the chain was forged. In reality, the founder of the Quaker movement was – and is, for it has to be discovered anew in each generation – The Holy Spirit.

It is difficult to give an idea of the origins of Quakerism in a few paragraphs. There were many people involved, from many differing levels of society. If I give a brief outline of the lives of two of the best known early Friends, it should not be thought that the lesser-known figures were less interesting. The lives of George Fox and William Penn, one a weaver's son with little education, the other the son of an admiral, well-educated and known at court, could not at first sight appear farther apart. Yet they shared the same inner revelation which led to their achievements in the world, and gave them the strength to overcome opposition.

George Fox

If George says 'verily' there is no altering him. (*Journal of George Fox*)

The seventeenth century was in many ways a time like our own. Great changes were taking place, and there

imprisonment. There is a story – possibly apocryphal – that illustrates the way in which the attitudes of early Friends could also be pragmatic. Because Penn moved in court circles, he was often called upon to dress in a way that he felt was inconsistent with his Quaker beliefs. This included wearing a sword. He asked George Fox about this, and Fox is said to have replied, 'Wear it as long as thou canst.'

William Penn is best known as the founder of Pennsylvania and Philadelphia, its capital, 'The City of Brotherly Love', was founded on Quaker principles. Penn's attitude towards the Native American tribes is one that illustrates the other side of the Quaker attitude to preaching the gospel. Though person-ally convinced of the teachings of Christ, he tried to see Christ within the tribal way of life. He approached Native Americans not as potential converts but in a spirit of Love, to learn what they had to teach him and to appreciate the fine example of their lives. He was also concerned to allow them the freedom to continue their traditional way of life. In this way he made friends with them, but did not try to make Friends of them.

Penn is also known for his trial at Newgate, when he asked the jury to stand by their verdict of 'not guilty' against a recorder who had ordered them to find the Quakers guilty. This they did, in spite of being bullied and locked up without food or drink. They were eventually fined and imprisoned, but they held on to their belief that the verdict should be decided according to the evidence. This trial is seen as a land-mark of English legal history, and eventually led to the establishment of the right of juries to give their verdict according to their convictions. It has been the subject of a number of films and plays.

Penn was also a mystic and visionary, and a writer whose works had a great impact on, among others, Robert Louis Stevenson who, it is said, kept his copy of *Some Fruits of Solitude* with him at all times. Another of Penn's books, *The Peace of Europe*, contains suggestions which we are only now, with the creation of the European Community, beginning to try to put into practice.

———————

There were two ways in which the seventeenth century was, in theory, very different from our own. The first was the absolute power of the monarch, and the second the absolute power of the Church. It went without saying that everyone was expected to accept the Christian faith as the only right one, but actually, in England, only one form of faith was permitted by law. This was the official faith of the monarch, and dissent was treason. Dissent also led to persecution. The more those in power try to suppress discussion, particularly on religion, the more takes place, and so it was that, even in the 1650s when Parliament or the Protector Cromwell were in power, Quakers and other dissenters were heavily persecuted.

The same powers that tried to prohibit discussion, also attempted to ban the publishing of books, pamphlets and journals which dissented from the prevailing view. They did not succeed. One of the reasons that we know so much about early Friends and their sufferings and struggles, their discoveries and their joys, is that Quakers completely ignored this prohibition. They published literally hundreds of publications of various kinds, most of which are still available to us today. Indeed, through their three hundred and fifty years of history, the number of publications by and about Quakers must run into many thousands, dealing with all aspects of Quaker life. This is a very important reason why Quakerism has survived.

The opponents of Quakerism could be highly vitriolic. Quakers today tend to speak gently about most things, though we can be very outspoken about something that we feel very strongly about. Early Friends had no such qualms. If the opposition framed their criticisms in words that were sarcastic, harsh and scornful, and condemned Quakers to hell and worse, they themselves matched word for word and were not known for suffering those they saw as fools (and worse) gladly.

It is good fun, as well as instructive, to look at the title pages of some seventeenth-century Quakeriana (and anti-Quakeriana). One of George Fox's works defending Quakerism has the following title page (capitals and spelling as original):

THE GREAT MYSTERY OF THE GREAT WHORE
UNFOLDED AND ANTICHRIST'S KINGDOM
Revealed unto DESTRUCTION
In Answer to many False Doctrines and Principles
which *Babylon's* Merchants have traded with, being held
forth by the professed Ministers, and Teachers and Professors
in *England, Ireland* and *Scotland*, taken under their owne
Hands, and from their owne Mouths, sent for by Them from
time to time, against the despised People of the LORD called
QUAKERS, who are the Seed of that Woman, who have
been long fled into the WILDERNESS.

Early Friends were not afraid to speak their truth strongly, and to trade insults with the Church or state.

———◆———

Do you welcome the diversity of culture, language and expressions of faith … [16]

One of the great insights of Quakerism is that the life of the spirit requires two languages: the language of silence and the language of words. Little can be said about the language of silence. It has to be experienced, and Quakers have discovered that the best way is in a group that has the specific intention of worshipping God. More will be said about the meeting for worship, prayer and meditation in a later chapter.

Throughout their existence as a separate body, Quakers have evolved their own language of words to describe their spiritual findings. This process continues today. Language has always been very important to Friends, and it still is. Because we are aware that it is vital to seek the spirit behind the words, it is particularly important that the words come as close to expressing the Spirit as possible. Meeting in silence, we know that words are inadequate to describe all that takes place there, but we also know that, if inspired, they have a value which is priceless.

Because we wish to describe our experiences in a way that will be strictly truthful to our experience, we sometimes use terms that are different – or familiar words in a different way. Phrases such as 'In the Life', 'concern' and 'speaking to my condition', are efforts to express clearly what is going on, and have been tested by time. Because there was no theological language in existence, and because Friends were generally not theologians anyway, they have tended to use ordinary terms in a special way to express clearly and simply what happens. Friends have always been willing to stretch the boundaries of spiritual language.

And language changes. Although today we continue to use some of the special terms – largely because we cannot find better words to express what we wish to convey, we are aware that the language of the spiritual life needs to be in tune with the times. Contemporary Quaker language strives to be non-sexist; not to imply prejudice in any way; and to be clearly understood by others who may not share our beliefs.

The Language of Your Inner Life

It can be helpful to look at the language that you use to express your spiritual life. Is it the same language that you use in everyday life, or do you have a special 'sacred language' for describing your relationship with God? It is not wrong to have such a special way of talking about our inner life, but it is also good to try to express it in everyday language, even if we only do it for ourselves. This exercise helps to close the gap which can arise between the spiritual and the everyday. The ideal is that the everyday is spiritual, and our language has an important part to play in that.

An exercise such as the one I describe below is very valuable. These days we can read the works of saints, masters, teachers and preachers from all over the world, from every world faith and tradition, and spanning thousands of years in time. We can see their lives in films, on television or on the stage, and because we have access to such a variety of language through the media and specialist books, we can easily become confused. It is important to decide on what we really value and believe, and to try to do so in our own language. George Fox, in one of his most quoted statements, said, 'Christ saith this, and the Apostles say that. But what canst thou say; is it from God?'[4]

I often advise people to take a single sheet of paper and try to write down clearly what they know – not believe – about their inner life. This helps in focussing on what is really essential. I suggest they re-read the sheet from time to time to help bring these truths to the surface of their lives and into their everyday world – and not to worry if it is not the same each time they do it. Change is essential to growth.

While we Quakers are clear that we have much to share with others, we also recognise that others have much to share with us – and that they may have better ways of expressing it. Today we may find additional spiritual inspiration outside the Society of Friends. This is not a rejection of our own tradition. In the *Advices and Queries* (*see* Appendix 1) which is a potted guide to the Quaker life, it is suggested that we learn to ' ... hear where words come from' and be ' ... open to fresh light from wherever it may come'. Remaining loyal to the traditions of silent contemplative worship, to our peace and social testimonies, and to the inspiration of other Friends, we feel free to use spiritual language gleaned from other sources if it expresses our experiences more clearly than traditional Christian terms. And there is also the unspoken language of the natural world and other aspects of creation that we can hear with our inner ears – if we are still enough.

When I became a Quaker I did not leave my Roman Catholicism or my Buddhism behind, but added them to the rich tradition I have inherited from early Friends. The same is true for many of us today. It is easy to say that we reject our previous faith and practice, but even then it remains there, as a part of us. Even if we reject its outer forms, we have to accept that it is a part of us, and that we would not be who we are, or where we are, without it.

We are fortunate to have access to the scriptures and other writings from all of the world's great faiths, as well as the inspirational works of poets and other writers. (I know that I said previously that they can cause confusion, but they can also be a great blessing.) Having been involved with other faiths for many years, I am greatly blessed by the freedom to use words or quotations from other traditions when I feel that they express more clearly what I wish to convey. And I have to admit that sometimes they do.

George Fox knew of the Qu'ran, and was able to quote from it when corresponding with Muslims.[5] In many other ways, he broke new ground in the language of the spiritual life of his day. He used metaphors for God that expressed how he found God operating in his life. He did call God 'The Lord', 'Christ' and 'Jesus' , but also used the terms 'The Light', ' The Seed' and 'The Guide' to speak of the Divine Presence. I cannot help but wonder what use he would have made of the tremendous variety of spiritual language available to us today.

———◆–◆–◆———

Each of us has a particular experience of God and each must find the way to be true to it [17]

Quaker belief and practice is as relevant to the life of today as to the seventeenth century. To see something of God in everyone – even if what this means is not clearly defined – helps to transform human relationships. To demonstrate that each person has the ability to listen to the God within themselves does not lessen faith, but adds a new dimension to it. Our lives can be governed in this way. We can all make direct contact with this Living Spirit for guidance and help, and in doing so we are set free from some of the problems of the spiritual life, those caused by priests, pastors, masters and gurus. This knowledge of God within us brings freedom, but also adds the discipline that keeps us from doing harm to others.

I have met many people who have been crippled by the abuses of religion. Some of them have turned to me for help. Because of my involvement with the Quaker tradition, I am able to point out that they have the answer within themselves, and to suggest ways they can find it. Some I send along to Quaker meetings. Others do not wish to approach any kind of group, since they feel that groups have been the cause of their problems. Either way, I have found that contact with a tradition that emphasises the Divine within them is a healing experience.

Early Friends found themselves touched by the Spirit which they found within the silence of meditation and worship. Today, many are touched in the same way by a Spirit that seems vastly different to that of the seventeenth century. Yet it is not. It is the same Spirit, though its manifestations are such as to meet the needs of today.

Quakers have a tradition of testifying strongly to the reality of the Spirit working in the world. In the past, this led to conflict with the powers of church and government. They voiced opposition to, for example, 'times and seasons' – saying that no day is more holy than any other. They refused the paying of tithes to church or state, because such tithes had been abolished in the New Testament. They were willing to go to prison for their beliefs. While such strong action may have been necessary for the time, Friends did not seek to be different for its own sake. They did feel that they were set apart from the world – in a similar way that a monastic order might be – but it was an inner state. They sought to be 'in the world but not of it', as they believed the early church had been.

Modern Friends are a part of the world we live in. We still retain the right to speak up for what we have discovered to be good and in harmony with our inner guidance. We do not usually go to extremes, though some Friends may feel they have to if they are up against a law or a power that they find unjust. An example might be those Friends who have to register as conscientious objectors in time of war, or some who feel they must not pay the portion of their taxes that is spent on armaments. We speak the truth as we have discovered it and as it relates to conditions in our world. These are what we call our 'testimonies'. They are driven by the power of the same Spirit, illumined by the Light within, and guided by the Still Small Voice. They have been confirmed as right by testing with our meetings and with other groups beyond our meetings. They exemplify our adherence to the basic message of Christ, to love our neighbour as ourselves.

The testimony that Friends in the modern world are best known for is that of our opposition to war and violence – and in this the Spirit that inspired early Friends is still the same – but it is not the only one. Other current Quaker testimonies include simplicity, the experiential nature of religious experience, inclusive language, and the importance of all people regardless of sex, race or social position. Our business meetings, which are conducted in a spirit of worship, and where there is no vote, also have much to say on the generally adversarial nature of the world's decision-making. Other organisations have found it helpful to borrow aspects of this and other Quaker ways of working. Our testimony that the truth should be spoken on all occasions led to our being allowed to affirm in court, instead of taking the oath. Affirming means that we declare that we tell the truth, not because we have invoked God as our witness, but because to tell the truth is an integral part of our lives as Quakers.

All this is a part of the Quaker way of life. Modern Friends are urged to, 'Be aware of the Spirit of God in the ordinary activities and experience of your daily life'.[7] This is still true, though in the present climate we may be reluctant to speak of it, for fear of being seen as 'different' or 'preachy'. We see ourselves as 'seekers' (a name given to the earliest groups in which the Quaker message found a home), but we have also made discoveries through the years of our existence, many of which can be helpful to people living today if they are known. That is the purpose of this book.

THE SOURCE

All of us need to find a way into silence which allows us
to deepen our awareness of the Divine ... [3]

In order to fully understand the Quaker way we need to
have knowledge – and preferably experience – of the
Quaker Meeting for Worship. It is probably the silent
worship that has attracted most of the Quakers who have
come from other traditions. We may not fully understand it
at the beginning, as I did not, but if it is right for us, something draws us back until we experience what it has to give
us. From the seventeenth century until the present day, it
remains the source from which everything else springs.

Put in the simplest possible way, a meeting for worship
occurs when two or more people come together to sit in
silence, and wait to experience the presence of God. The term
is most often used to describe what occurs in a Quaker
meeting house, usually on a Sunday morning. But it can
happen anywhere or at any time. Although silence is the basis

of a meeting for worship, anyone present is permitted to speak if they feel moved to do so. Such speaking is called 'ministry'. We will return to this later.

The Meeting for Worship is full of paradox. Outwardly simple, the more we participate in it the more we become aware of a great deal happening inwardly, both to the individual and to the group. Silent, yet the deepest insights may come when a member of the meeting is moved to speak, even though the words may not be very profound in themselves. The idea of God that is worshipped may be different to each person present, yet in the silence there is a Unity that is beyond words and thoughts. It is our greatest source of strength, yet one which we find difficult to speak about or describe. The experience of this new kind of silence has been a turning point for many of us, yet we may find it impossible to explain why to our friends and relatives. It is *the* great unifying factor among Friends, but can be the cause of division within households, if it becomes very important for one member, while others find nothing they can share.

----•◆•----

Don't feel restricted by the silence, it is there to set you free from the pressures of life … Freedom of expression is the freedom to worship God on your own terms. Value the opportunity to think unguided by the world. Learn what you feel you need to know, let other information pass. No moment of silence is a waste of time.
(Rachel Needham, 1987, *Quaker Faith and Practice*
QFP, 2. 17)

The best starting point might be to describe the outward experience first. A group of people, which may vary from two or three to many hundreds, come together in a room – any room – and sit quietly. They come with the expectation of finding God's presence. They do not have any special clothing or other outward identification, neither do they sit in any special places. They do not have a uniform posture, as a group of meditators might have, for some may sit up straight, while others slump in various positions. D T Suzuki, the famous writer on Zen Buddhism, was once taken to a Quaker meeting. Used to the upright posture of groups of Zen meditators, he was reported to have been horrified at that of the worshippers!

I said that the meeting for worship can take place in 'any room', and this is indeed so. Most religious systems have a concept of 'sacred space'. Churches, temples and other buildings dedicated to worship are blessed or consecrated. For Quakers, sacred space is created by the intention to meet together to experience the presence of God. It comes from within the worshippers. This is symbolised – albeit unconsciously – by the fact that most Quaker meetings now place the chairs in a circle or square.

There are old meeting houses where the prayer of over three hundred years seems to have soaked into the fabric of the building. This is of course true of old churches and temples everywhere, but Friends often seem curiously reluctant to acknowledge the help given to the meeting by being in a place that has been used for worship for so long. I recently gave a talk at a meeting-house built in 1657, and it was amazing how quickly all of us were able to settle into a deep stillness where the Presence of God was very real.

The meeting starts when the first person goes into the meeting-room and sits down quietly. The seating arrangements usually mean that the worshippers face each other. Quaker worship is very much a group activity, and awareness of the other worshippers is a vital part of the process. The meeting closes, usually after an hour, when two members shake hands. These are usually elders of the meeting, but any two people may be appointed for this purpose.

A friend of mine – not a Quaker – once said, 'It's like a waiting room.' And, in some senses, that is what it is. Viewed from the outside, the gathering can seem more like a waiting room than a church. The inner experience, the essence of the Quaker meeting for worship, can be summed up in the three words, 'Waiting on God'.

———— ◆ ————

Words split apart, Silence unites. Words scatter, Silence gathers together. Words stir up, Silence brings peace. Words engender denial, Silence invites even the denier to find fresh hope in the confident expectation of a mystery which can be accomplished within. In my active silence, I shall prepare myself to hear the Silence of God.
(Pierre Lacout, *God is Silence*)

Let us pause for a minute and consider what we mean by 'God'. There is probably no word in the English – or any other – language that means so many different things to different people. Certainly in any Quaker meeting today you will find a wide range of theological views. Yet if we are going to meet to worship God, then the question of what kind of God we are worshipping is of great importance.

Let us just consider some of the possibilities. At one end of the spectrum there are those who believe that God is the Creator, and that He created all that exists. He is revealed as our Father by Jesus, who is the Son of God. The teachings of Jesus about God, as well as the other teachings essential to our spiritual welfare, are to be found in the Bible. At the other end there are those who consider that God is essentially unknowable, infinite, eternal, a Universal Force. There are also those who are agnostic; they say that they are not even sure as to whether anyone or anything that they could call God actually exists. Yet they have an inner urge to go on seeking, and they experience something in the silent meeting which they cannot – as yet – put into words.

Some Quakers question whether such seekers should be allowed to become members. Yet we know that the earliest Friends were called 'Seekers after Truth'. In the Silence, it seems that such questions do not matter. It is only when words and thoughts – 'notions' as they were called by George Fox – creep in that these questions are seen as important. This is the great paradox of Quakers today. Differences that would split most groups into a thousand fragmented individuals are reconciled and accepted in the silence.

God is Silence. God is also an infinite number of other things. One of the greatest discoveries of Quakers is that in that deep stillness where there is a profound unity, differences of words and concepts no longer matter. In the spirit of the silence and the depths of listening to it, God will be there for us in a way that will meet our needs, both as individuals and as a community.

———◆◆◆———

Do you respect that of God in everyone though it
may be expressed in unfamiliar ways or be difficult
to discern? (17)

Most Christian groups refer to the Divine portion of our being as the Soul. Quakers do not use this word, but instead talk about 'That of God' within each of us. The phrase comes from George Fox. It is used several times in his *Journal*, but the one most quoted comes in a letter to Friends written in 1656, in which he urges them to:

> … be patterns, be examples in all countries, places, is-
> lands, nations, wherever you come; that your carriage and
> life may preach among all sorts of people, and to them.
> Then you will come to walk cheerfully over the world,
> answering *that of God* in every one; whereby in them ye
> may be a blessing, and make the witness of God in them
> to bless you.[6]

Note that his emphasis is on living the spiritual life, rather than preaching. It is interesting that whatever 'That of God' is seen to be, it is certainly something that enables us to bless others and receive blessings from them.

Though Friends do not readily define 'That of God', it is one of the central tenets in living our lives. We know what it means, and feel that this simple phrase clearly expresses the Divine in everyone. So we hesitate to put it into other terms. If we accept the Divine within ourselves, we will feel able to turn to it for guidance. If we recognise it in others, we automatically set them free, and will not want to interfere in their lives in a negative way.

———◆———

Take heed, dear Friends, to the promptings of love and truth in your hearts. Trust them as the leadings of God whose Light shows us our darkness and brings us to new life. [1]

Another key concept when Friends talk about God is that of 'The Inward Light'. Modern Quaker writings tend to talk about 'The Inner Light', and there are differences of opinion as to whether they are the same. George Fox does not use 'inner' at all. The term he and other early Friends used is 'Inward'. If there is a difference it is that thinking about 'inner' and 'outer' creates a dualism, whereas to refer to the Light as 'inward' has overtones of direction, and points us to The Kingdom of Heaven within. Awareness of such a difference helps to guide our seeking and our prayer life, and helps us to discover the Oneness.

This Light *is* 'That of God' within each person (and some would say within all created things). Or, put another way, 'That of God' and the Light are One. This Light is the Light of Christ, and is equated with what St Paul called 'The Mind of Christ'. Others see it as Life, which like Light is freely given to all creation. We know the Light as the Unconditional Love of God which, if we can accept it, we are able to radiate as light to the world around us.

The Light is seen in different ways. Paradoxically, we do not often talk about 'seeing' it. The way in which we are most aware of it is through what the Bible calls 'the Still Small Voice'. Others in different traditions have called it 'The Voice of the Silence', 'The Unstruck Music' or 'the Word'. In this intuitive whisper we are enabled to discover the will of God for us, and then we 'see' the Light as we listen to it guiding us.

Light is a very important Universal symbol. It is not limited to Quakers, but we use it in a very specific way, as another name for Christ, the Divine within all creation. It is found as a symbol for the Divine in all world religions, and in all mystical traditions. It is seen in the earliest written records of spiritual experience, from ancient Egypt, India and Persia, through Hinduism, Judaism, Christianity and Islam to the present day. Sometimes the Light is seen as a peaceful symbol, gently showing the way ahead, or filling us with wisdom and healing, and sometimes it is the fire which burns up all the old self, to allow the Divine to manifest.

Experience of the Light is something that does not come to us through scriptures. The mystics of all traditions have the ability to pass it on – or rather to awaken it in others by recognising that it is there in all creation. This can also occur in the Quaker Meeting for Worship. Sometimes the Light is personified, as with Christ as The Light of the World, or

Amitabha, the Buddha of Infinite Light in the Buddhist tradition. At other times it is impersonal, leading us to the point where all projections disappear.

———◆———

Bring the whole of your life under the ordering of the
spirit of Christ. ... Remember that Christianity is not a
notion but a way. [2]

The Light is also 'The Guide' when it assumes a personal aspect for us. It is the 'Inner teacher', or 'Christ in us'. The Light enables us to see the *Way* (another synonym for Christ), and follow the way which is the right one for us in harmony with God's will. It is essentially loving, but can be quite uncompromising in showing us where we have gone wrong. The Light not only dissolves the darkness, but it also shows us if we are walking a path that is not in harmony with the teachings of Christ. It is always said that before we awaken this Light within us, we have to be sure that we are willing to follow it. Life may lead us through suffering, but because the Guide has the nature of Love, all will be well in the end. Luke Cock, an early Yorkshire Friend and a butcher by trade, illustrated this with rich symbolism and local dialect in a sermon he gave in 1721.

I remember when I first met with my Guide. He led me to
a very large and cross (place) where I was to speak the
truth from my heart. 'Nay then,' said I to my Guide,
'I mun leave Thee here: if Thou leads me up that lane, I
can never follow: I'se be ruined of this butchering trade, if I

mun't lie for a gain.' Here I left my Guide, and was filled
with sorrow, and went back to the Weeping Cross: and I
said, 'If I could find my Good Guide again, I'll follow him,
lead me wither he will.' So here I found my Guide again,
and began to follow him up this lane and tell the Truth
from my heart. I had been nought but beggary and poverty
before, and now I began to thrive at my trade, and got to
the end of this lane, though with some difficulty. [7]

And he went on to tell of the other lanes along which his
guide led him, and of the sorrows and joys that following the
guide brought him.

Contrast this with a contemporary Friend, who reflects the
uncertain spirit of today, yet who finds the same degree of
certainty that there is a source from which comfort and guidance can be drawn.

The people whom I know who live a truly non-violent life
are in touch with the source of power, call it what you will;
The Light, the seed, God, the holy spirit. Many others of
us find this well-spring when we need it, and lose it again,
find it and lose it, find it and lose it. When I have something very difficult to face that I know I can't cope with,
then I turn desperately to the source. One of the things I
find most infuriating about myself is that I often let the
contact go when the emergency is over and flounder along
without it for months on end when my everyday existence
could be transformed by it ...

More than anything I want to learn to live in the Light.
So I think, anyway, but in fact I perhaps don't altogether
want to take the demands involved, don't want to see all
the dust in my life. [8]

Throughout history there have been many – not only Quakers – who have followed this Light and Guide, and none have ever claimed that it is easy. Another name for it is conscience, a word that is not very popular these days. Yet Friends and others have found that following it is the most worthwhile thing that we can do, for it leads to a wholeness that is hard – if not impossible – to find in any other way.

The Religious Society of Friends is rooted in Christianity and has always found inspiration in the life and teachings of Jesus. [4]

Quakers have also identified this Light with Jesus. We are quite clear that Quakerism grew out of a new vision of the life and teaching of Jesus, and the importance of these has never been lost. The revelation of George Fox that 'There is one, even Christ Jesus, that can speak to thy condition' and the confirming testimony of many Friends through the years emphasises this importance.

Some British Quakers today are orthodox in their Christian beliefs, having a real and vivid experience of salvation through the death and resurrection of Jesus. Others would be reluctant to put it that way, but there is no doubt that Jesus is a central figure in the lives of most Quakers. For Friends in other countries, such as Kenya and parts of the USA, Jesus is definitely seen as the Son of God and the Redeemer of humankind.

However, most Friends would agree that the important thing is Jesus's life and teachings. A Christian is one who tries to follow the teachings of Jesus, rather than putting him on an altar to worship.

> Not everyone that saith to me, Lord Lord, shall enter the
> Kingdom of Heaven, but he that doth the will of my
> Father which is in Heaven [9]

is a teaching that Quakers take seriously.

———— ◆·◆·◆ ————

> We seek a gathered stillness in our meetings for worship
> so that all may feel the power of God's love drawing us
> together and leading us. [8]

This idea of waiting on God may appear simple, but it is by no means easy. It takes practice. As anyone who has tried meditation will know, the moment we try to sit quietly and allow our minds to settle, seems to be the moment our minds run riot with thoughts. The more we try to be silent, or to concentrate on matters relating to the spiritual life, the more the mind – 'the monkey mind' as Hindus call it – behaves just like a restless monkey, swinging aimlessly from branch to branch.

John Edward Southall, a nineteenth-century Quaker printer, would not have put it that way, but he knew the same experience. He relates how he had read that God was waiting in the depths of his being to talk to him, if only he would become still enough to hear. He thought this would be very easy, but:

... I had no sooner commenced than a perfect pandemonium of voices reached my ears, a thousand clamouring notes from without and within, until I could hear nothing but their noise and din ... Then came the conflicts of thoughts for the morrow, but God said, 'Be Still'. And as I listened, and slowly learned to obey, and shut my ears to every sound, I found, after a while, that when other voices ceased, or I ceased to hear them, there was a still small voice in the depths of my being that began to speak with an inexpressible tenderness, power and comfort. [10]

As you can see, this is no new phenomenon.

In the meeting for worship we, like John Edward Southall, may start by trying to think thoughts of God, in order to provide a space where we can listen to the 'still small voice' through which God within us speaks. We may have to bring our minds back to the subject time after time. When a strong feeling of oneness with God and with each person present develops, the meeting is said to have 'gathered'. This process can have an amazing effect. The distracting thought-voices and the activity of the 'monkey-mind' become still, in a way that we can neither anticipate nor achieve by our own efforts.

———◦◦◦———

Yield yourself and all your outward concerns to God's guidance so that you may find 'the evil weakening in you and the good raised up'. [9]

Seventeenth-century Friends tended to be extravagant in their language. There is no doubt that what they experienced in worship was a real and powerful force. They had the same difficulties as later Friends, and they were more accepting of the power of God's help in overcoming them. Robert Barclay, probably the first Quaker theologian, said of his early experience of Meeting:

> When I came into the silent assemblies of God's people, I felt a secret power among them, which touched my heart, and as I gave way to it, I found the evil weakening in me and the good raised up ... ' [11]

Francis Howgill told how, in his experience:

> The Lord of heaven and earth we each found to be near at hand as we waited upon Him in pure silence. [12]

Thomas Story waxed even more poetic:

> ... after I had sat down among them, that heavenly and watery cloud over-shadowing my mind brake into a sweet abounding shower of celestial rain. [13]

Contemporary Quakers might hesitate to use such language, but our experience is just as real.

A more recent description is given by Caroline Stephen, the aunt of the novelist Virginia Woolf, and Friends today can easily identify with her words:

> One never-to-be-forgotten Sunday morning, I found my-self one of a small company of silent worshippers who

were content to sit together without words, that each
one might feel after and draw near to the Divine
Presence, unhindered at least, if not helped, by any
human utterance. Utterance I knew was free, should the
words be given; and before the meeting was over, a sentence or two were uttered with great simplicity by an
old and apparently untaught man, rising in his place
among the rest of us. I did not pay much attention to
the words he spoke and I have no recollection of their
purport. My whole soul was filled with the unutterable
peace of the undisturbed opportunity for communion
with God, with the sense that at last I have found a
place where I might, without the faintest suspicion of
insincerity, join with others in simply seeking His presence. To sit in silence could at least pledge me to
nothing; it might open to me (as it did that morning)
the very gate of heaven. [14]

This 'gathering' as Quakers call it, this coming together in
deep peace, this opening of Heaven's gate and the resultant
feeling of the reality of God's presence, is the heart of the
worship. Whether or not anyone speaks, this is a time
beyond words, thoughts and ideas, when the mind is still,
and God is known to be a living reality. This is a truly
mystical path.

Some Quakers, however, are reluctant to call their path a
mystical one in case it implies that their experience is
entirely other-worldly, only given to a chosen few, and not
available to all. As we shall see, such an experiential way of
worship is not the exclusive property of Quakers, but can
be practised by any group who set their hearts and minds
on doing it. Quakers have been practising it for over three

hundred years which gives a validity to their experience. Our message to today's world is that such a thing is possible, and that it does not need special places or people to bring it about.

———◆———

When prompted to speak, wait patiently to know that the leading and the time are right, but do not let a sense of your own unworthiness hold you back. [13]

Should someone be moved to speak, their speech does not break the silence. It may seem to, but it does not. It is as if the silence is a flowing current; the stream on which the ministry flows. What is said may not seem relevant to you, but it may have real meaning for others present. It is a familiar experience that good ministry (and let us be honest, the other kind does exist) can answer unspoken questions, or shed light on deep problems, without them ever having been mentioned or expressed in any way. Examples occur too regularly for this to be a coincidence, and most regular worshippers will have experienced it happening to them. It does not matter whether it is everyday problems, such as trouble within the family, or spiritual difficulties, such as doubt over one of the Quaker testimonies. Problems may be theological, related to the nature of God or the causes of suffering in the world, or someone may be going through a personal 'Dark night of the soul'. All these needs and many more have been met through the ministry of words that come out of a gathered silence.

I remember coming to Meeting with the problems of a close relative active in my mind. I could not keep my thoughts on anything else, and was becoming resigned that this was to be one of those meetings – they do happen – when, try as I might, I would not feel a part of the spiritual experience of that hour. Suddenly, there was a great feeling of hush, in which the noises from outside and inside the meeting-house seemed to be dampened. Then a Friend, who was visiting for the day, and whom I therefore did not know, stood up and spoke. She told the story of having gone through a similar problem to my relative, and of its solution. The remainder of that hour was one of the most deeply gathered meetings that I have ever known. Many Quakers can tell a similar tale.

The experience of really being moved to minister is a strange one. Some Friends tell of being impelled on to their feet, with no knowledge of why this is happening. My personal experience is of feeling moved to stand, with just a sentence or part of one in my mind. And I am often unaware of the next sentence until I have spoken the first. The subject may turn out to be something unrelated to the thoughts that had been in my mind earlier in the meeting. It is a very odd feeling, slightly disorientating, and it is often hard to remember what I have said. Another way ministry can happen is when a thought slowly grows and develops through the silence, until it becomes so strong that I am compelled to share it. Occasionally, there is a feeling of trembling, which, some say, is related to the way Quakers got their name.

Are you open to the healing power of God's Love?
Cherish that of God within you, so that this love may
grow in you and guide you [2]

Within the silence of the meeting there is great healing. There have been reports of physical healings following regular attendance at meetings. Early Friends expected such things to happen when, as George Fox often put it, 'the Power of the Lord was over all' and it was experienced by everyone in the meeting. However, meeting for worship is not primarily a meeting for healing, though some Quakers do hold special meetings for this purpose. Nor is it for counselling, advice or political or social statements. Healing, inspiration and peace of mind are fruits of the search for God and the experience of the Divine Presence. Quaker experience confirms the words of Jesus: 'Seek first the Kingdom of God, and all else will be added unto you.' [15]

One of the questions I am most often asked – by both Quakers and non-Quakers – is: 'Do you think the Meeting for worship is a form of meditation?' The main problem is that there are so many different ideas on what is meditation itself. If meditation is seen as a method or technique of individual spiritual development or self-realisation, then it probably is not the same as Quaker worship. If it is a seeking of the presence of God within, then it is. However, meeting for worship is a seeking for the Presence of God with the group. One Friend expressed it this way: 'We listen to each others' silence.' And this aspect is not found within most of the current teaching on meditation.

One might equally ask if Quaker worship is the same as a service of Holy Communion, a Buddhist or Hindu *puja* or any other form of ritual worship. In many ways Quaker Worship is actually closer to these. For many people ritual worship is also an act of meditation. In order to have conscious worship, the presence of the god or other object of worship has to be realised. Many forms of religious meditation picture the god-form – Christ, Krishna or Buddha for example – as dwelling within the heart of the worshipper. Quakers do not have any images in their place of worship, but because they believe that there is 'that of God' within everyone, they may carry an image of God within themselves. This Divine presence is found in a silent searching within. It is no less real for the absence of outward signs and symbols.

A major aspect of worship in most of the world's traditions is of an offering of some kind being a part of the service. In a Quaker meeting there is no outward offering. A Quaker meeting is above all an offering of our hearts and minds to God. It is prayer. (The old Roman Catholic Catechism defined prayer as ' ... the raising up of the mind and heart to God.') That is one of the reasons why the term 'worship' is used.

As we come to know God as Light and Love within our deepest self, we automatically radiate that awareness to others. It happens in spite of ourselves. In this way, Divine Grace enhances the ability of all present to experience it beyond their personal capacity. Worship is the experience of grace or, in other language, the descent of the Holy Spirit. Awareness of this generates a deep feeling of reverence, which grows until the meeting is fully gathered. All become aware of something greater, a deep Reality (whatever name they may give it) that takes over the meeting. The meeting moves through various stages to this deep climax regardless of the absence of ritual, singing or chanting, much like any liturgical form of worship. The great difference is that the 'order of service' is neither programmed nor certain. It takes place – when it does – in God's time, not ours.

This apparent absence of structure and ritual – though we do have our rituals – can cause problems. Quakers are human, and today we are a part of this new educated world. When we emerge from this deep and unifying experience, we try to express it in words, and this is where difficulties arise. These are mostly theological. Many Friends today are refugees from other churches where they may have had bad experiences, and felt that they were not understood. They may find orthodox Christian language repellent. Others come wishing to add Quaker life and experience to their orthodox Christian faith. (There are Quakers in 'dual membership' who attend other forms of worship or practice in addition to the Quaker meeting.) All this leads at best to a rich tapestry of discussion; at worst to a tower of Babel where new hurts and misunderstandings may be generated.

In order to reach the experience of a gathered meeting, individual Quakers have their own techniques. (Some Friends will object to the use of the word 'technique' in relation to their beloved meeting, but recent surveys have shown that techniques are used by many Friends.) Those who were born into Quakerism tended to absorb the way of worship by a sort of 'osmosis'. But, today, most Quakers have come from outside the Society of Friends, and they need a 'way' to help them centre down in meetings.

Many start by thinking about a passage from the Bible or other inspirational writings that they may have read during the week. Others have a simple approach of praying or talking to God, while still others may use one of the well-known techniques of meditation such as watching the breath or use of a repeated word or phrase. I know Friends who spend the first part of a meeting looking round at each one present, and invoking a blessing for them. I know others who look out of the window, or at the flowers in the centre. (British Quaker meetings usually have a table in the centre of the chairs, on which are placed some flowers, Bibles and copies of *Quaker Faith and Practice*. Silent meetings in the USA and elsewhere do not.)

Whatever technique may be used, all agree that it is not the essence of the worship, but only a preliminary to help the mind to become focused on the true purpose of the meeting, openness to the reality of God within. The problem with techniques is that they are something that we feel we have to *do*, and there is a temptation to practise them with concentrated effort. The ideal attitude is a relaxed openness to all that is going on and to the other members of the meeting. This allows the power of the spirit to flow into our worship, and to take us beyond our own limitations. If we use a technique, then it should be with the sole aim of helping us to relax into the silence. As soon as the mind becomes relatively still, we surrender to the power of the silence to take us even deeper.

The experience of the gathered meeting is something that is given by grace. That is to say, it is a gift from the Divine. We do not earn it by our efforts, and we cannot guarantee that it will happen, but we do have to be able to receive it. And we have to prepare ourselves to receive it. The awareness of it individually is directly related to our willingness to share it. The Spirit of God cannot be commanded. But when we experience It as Love, and are willing to share It, not only with other members of the meeting, but with the whole world, then we are given the grace and the power to do so. This is the Quaker experience. This is why the Quaker Meeting for Worship is seen by Friends as the source of their work in the world.

Another way in which meeting for worship differs from meditation is in the way Quakers worship as a community. After a gathered meeting we feel more a part of the community of Friends that every Quaker meeting should be. It is a very subtle thing, but one of the purposes of the Meeting for Worship is to weld together those present in a deep and loving way. And this experience is shared by many Friends.

The silence of Quaker worship does not end with the close of the meeting. The practice of worship helps us to bring silence into our everyday lives. It is the silence of 'prayer without ceasing'. Pierre Lacout, a Carmelite priest who was also a Friend, suggests that silence is so important in daily life that we should pray, 'Give us this day our daily silence.'[16] In return, the daily practice of times of stillness in our lives prepares us for the experience of worship. And so the wheel turns full circle, and our lives increasingly become an expression of the spirit of silent worship.

'Where two or three are gathered ... ' there is the Presence of God. This is the teaching of Jesus. It is no coincidence that early Friends used the term 'gathered' for a meeting that was at one in the experience of this Presence. The gathered meeting confirms this teaching and makes it a living reality. It extends this reality into our everyday life. The Presence of God is here all the time, and not just at times of spiritual seeking. Meeting with others for the common cause of worshipping God allows us to experience this as a vital truth, particularly at times when our relationships with others may be difficult. This is the true meaning of worship in everyday life.

If you want to go to an established Quaker meeting, you will be welcome. All Quaker meetings for worship are open to everyone. You can find the address by looking in the telephone book under 'Friends Meeting House', 'Quaker' or '(Religious) Society of Friends', or by writing or phoning Friends House (*see* Useful Addresses) to check the times of the meetings. You do not have to let anyone know you are coming, and it is up to you whether you speak to anyone there. Some people like to just go quietly on the first occasion, to be an observer. If that is what suits your temperament, that is all right. However, you may well find that there is someone at the door who greets everyone as they arrive.

If you say that this is your first meeting, you may be handed a copy of one or more leaflets which describe the meeting. Remember that the meeting starts when the first person goes in and sits in silence. Start by trying to think thoughts of God, in whatever way is helpful to you, and this will provide space in which you can 'listen' within yourself. You will have read earlier that Quakers believe that God within us can speak to us, and so this attitude of inner listening is the best way to move into the silence of the worship. You may have to bring your mind back to the subject repeatedly. Just do it gently; do not strain, or feel guilty if you are unable to hold God-thoughts or the listening attitude for more than a few minutes. When the meeting 'gathers', you will find that you are drawn into the silence in a way that you could neither anticipate nor achieve by your own efforts.

This process can have an amazing effect. Not only are you able to find peace in the meeting in a way that you had not thought possible, but you will find that this peace can be recalled later, when the world and its pressures crowd in on you. This may not happen on the first occasion, but if you persevere with Meeting then the peace and inspiration that it leaves with you soon become apparent. You have begun listening to the Light.

If you do not feel able to go to an established meeting, but you would like to experiment for yourself, then much of the above applies. Find one or more sympathetic friends who you can work with. Turn off the television, radio, the telephone and any other distractions, and set aside at least half an hour. Sit in a circle, or facing each other, and allow your mind to dwell on thoughts of the Divine.

Remember the words of Jesus: 'Where two or three are gathered together, there am I in the midst of them.'[17] He was speaking from his Divine centre, and you can safely take them as your authority. This will prepare you to experience the presence of God with you. Allow your mind to drift gently, keeping the thoughts of God uppermost. Do not strain or try too hard. You should be relaxed but alert. Remember the listening attitude referred to above.

As was mentioned earlier, ministry is an important part of Quaker worship. If anyone present feels moved to speak and share a thought or a prayer, that is good. It is helpful if people are prepared to wait a while to see if the impulse is real. If it is, do not be afraid that it will break the silence. The silence will flow though it, and it will give a focus which will lead to a deeper quiet. And it may turn out to be of greater help than you know to someone present.

A final word: every Meeting for Worship is an experiment. No two are the same. Whether you attend an existing meeting, where you have the advantage of Quakers with years of experience, or whether you experiment on your own, bear in mind that the purpose of the meeting is to become aware of the Presence of God. Everything else is secondary. Don't expect too much from any one meeting, but be open to whatever may come to you. Changes may begin to occur in your life as you extend the influence of meeting in this way into the everyday world. And above all, keep it simple and natural.

PERSONAL PRACTICE

Do you try to set aside times of quiet for openness to the
Holy Spirit? ... Do you encourage in yourself and in
others a habit of dependence on God's guidance for
each day? [4]

Quakers today have a variety of spiritual practices
which may come, as often as not, from outside our
own tradition. Because Friends have the guidance to be open
to fresh light from wherever it may come, it may be that we
are more open to new ideas. Whatever the reason, we do
find a great variety of personal spiritual practices among
Friends. Among those that I have encountered are meditation of various kinds, prayer, visualisation, circle dancing
and spiritual reading; journal writing – which includes
poetry, Bible study (Quaker style); music, both playing and
listening; spiritual friendships, retreats and various spiritual
healing practices.

Meditation and Prayer

S ilent worship provides the principle source from which Quakers draw their strength, but there is also a long Quaker tradition of personal prayer and meditation. Early Friends were clear about prayer, and though I don't think they used the word meditation very much, they certainly practised it. For example, although neither the words meditation nor contemplation appear in George Fox's *Journal*, there are frequent exhortations to 'mind the Light', 'feel the Light', and 'dwell in the Light'. There are references to 'the Inward Voice' of God and Christ; instructions to 'Wait upon the Lord whatever condition you may be in', and to wait 'in the Grace and Truth'.

This attention to the Light through watching and inner listening is the essence of the Quaker approach to meditation. Many would hesitate to call it meditation, because this word has so many meanings today, and some would think of it as prayer. It does not really matter what we call it. The simple process of inward listening or looking – depending on our temperament – has proved itself through the years to be sufficient for all needs, *if it is practised*. It has a depth that is as profound as any spiritual practice from any tradition.

There is a tendency today to judge the depth of spiritual practice by its complexity but, in fact, the reverse is often the case. Some of the deepest and most profound of spiritual teachings are contained in small books or pamphlets, or, when expanded, consist of saying the same direct thing in many different ways. Practical examples are Brother Lawrence's *Practice of the Presence of God*, or that modern Quaker classic quoted earlier, *God is Silence*. What Quakers are actually practising, even in their worship, is often called contemplative meditation.

Sometimes we too easily look elsewhere for guidance, and forget the beauty of our own tradition, or feel that its simple practice is not adequate for all the problems that arise in this modern world. This is a pity. In my experience it is not that the tradition is lacking, but that it has not properly been tried. To go into a meeting for worship and to truly surrender oneself to the Presence of God, can have an effect on one's spiritual life that is the equal of any other practice. This is also true of a willingness to wait upon God in our own homes, either with friends or family, or on our own. It requires patience, and the willingness to seek God first, and not to look for results for their own sake. We cannot truly know what is good for us or for others, but the spirit of 'Thy Will be done' has always been the essence of Quakerism. And it works.

———————

Are you open to new light, from whatever source it may come? Do you approach new ideas with discernment? [7]

In my spiritual life – and in this book – I am happy to draw on writings and teachings from other traditions where they express what I need to say, and where I do not have a suitable quotation from Quaker sources. Using such quotations does not detract from the Quaker way. In fact, it adds to it, for it shows that the principles discovered by Quakers through the years have a universal application. In the same way, Quakers have drawn on other traditions for their personal spiritual practice. I would like to take you on a journey through those that I know of, either from personal practice, or from the accounts of people that I have been fortunate enough to share part of my spiritual journey with, and whose accounts I trust. If I miss some out, it is because I cannot personally testify to their effectiveness, as I have not tried them. It is not because that effectiveness is in doubt.

Other Forms of Meditation

I have already looked at the traditional Quaker approach to meditation and this, in one form or another, is the most common among Friends. Nevertheless, other practices, drawn from traditions outside Quakerism, have been adopted in recent years by some Friends. At first, they were just used to help the centring down process in meeting for worship, but later Friends discovered their value in everyday life. In the section on worship, I spoke of the 'monkey mind', the oriental parable of the state of our minds when we try to still them. Some of these meditation techniques are used in the East to provide a branch where the monkey will feel able to rest. They include TM (Transcendental Meditation) and other forms of *mantra* meditation, Buddhist *samatha* meditation, and Zen.

One of the most widespread ways used to still the mind is the repetition of a mantra. A mantra is a word or phrase which is repeated over and over again until the mind becomes quiet. This kind of meditation is found within all the great spiritual traditions of the world. In Hinduism and Islam one of the names of God is usually used; in Buddhism, one of the names of Buddha. A mantra can also be a word given by a teacher, often one which has no precise meaning in English. A modern form, and one which attracted many Friends because it claims not to be religious in nature, is the Transcendental Meditation of the Maharishi Mahesh Yogi, best known for being the teacher of the Beatles.

There are also Christian traditions which are similar. Apart from the well known 'Jesus Prayer' of the Orthodox Churches where the name of Jesus is used as a mantra, there is the advice from the anonymous writer of *The Cloud of Unknowing* to take a short word and repeat it until the mind becomes still. Other contemporary teachings are the *Centering Prayer*, in which a short word or phrase is repeated slowly and contemplatively, and the form of Christian meditation taught by Father John Main of the Christian Meditation Movement which use the single Aramaic word, *Maranatha*, which means 'Come Lord [Jesus]'.

All these are based on a similar principle. As we focus the mind on one word or short phrase, the mind becomes saturated with the spiritual idea contained in it, and moves slowly to a state of one-pointedness where thoughts of God remain uninterrupted. From our concentration on saying the mantra, comes a state where the mantra seems to be saying itself, and we are observers. This is called 'letting the mind move into the heart', and is the goal of this type of meditation. When this happens, we are said to be in the state that St Paul called praying without ceasing.

Another approach to meditation that has proved helpful to Friends is drawn from Buddhist sources. Although Buddhism as a religion does not make use of ideas of God, its meditation techniques are very effective in bringing the mind to a state of stillness. Being wordless, they also tend to be more helpful because they do not add thoughts and concepts to the mental process. One of these practices is known as *samatha*, the practice of mindfulness of breathing. This is not a breathing exercise, but a simple observation of the breath's rise and fall. It can be observed either at the tip of the nose, or at the diaphragm. This practice brings the mind to a state of stillness very quickly, or at least, to a state where passing thoughts are seen as just that, and are no longer a problem. A variation involves counting the breaths.

Zen Buddhism holds quite a fascination for Quakers. It is iconoclastic, after the manner of early Friends, and it seeks direct spiritual experience. At the same time, it claims to be 'nothing special', and sees the spiritual life and the everyday life as being one. The practice of Zen has tended to become formalised, but its essence consists of 'just sitting' and reflecting upon our basic Buddha Nature. (Another name for the Inward Light) There are Friends both in Europe and the USA who also practise formal Zen meditation, and find that this daily practice complements the meeting for worship.

Formal practice of this type is not for everyone, and is outside the scope of this book. However, a developed awareness of ourselves when we are sitting in worship is a help to steadying the mind, and can be practised anywhere and at any time. Sit upright, feet flat on the floor and hands on your lap, and feel the sense of balance and poise that this posture brings. This way of sitting is likened to the Buddha image, which is in itself a symbol of inner peace. Simple awareness enables us to return to our roots, and to recognise the essential nature of the quiet mind, from which all other thoughts and inspirations can arise. It is the basic simplicity of the practice that is the key to its effectiveness, and also to its ready acceptance by some Friends.

Spiritual Reading

Remember the importance of the Bible, the writings of Friends and all writings which reveal the ways of God. [5]

There are other spiritual practices which are more natural to Friends, and the most natural of all is spiritual reading. Quakers are great readers – which is just as well since they have written and published so much material – but modern Friends do not only read Quaker publications. When I was manager of the Friends Book Centre in London, we used to sell a wide range of spiritual literature to members of the Yearly Meeting. The writings of the Catholic mystics were very popular, with new editions of *Practice of the Presence of God*, *The Cloud of Unknowing* and the writings of Saint Theresa of

Avila eagerly seized upon. We were one of the first bookshops to import the works of Anthony de Mello from India. Friends also bought material from other faiths. Writings on Vedanta and Buddhism were particularly popular, as were those on Zen, its radical and humorous approach having a particular appeal.

The art of spiritual reading is a very old one. It is part of the traditional 'Lectio Divina' of the early Christian church. It is interesting that Friends, who thought of themselves as restoring primitive Christianity, should have encouraged the written word, seeing it as an essential part of their teachings. The importance that they gave it is highlighted in the fact that some early Quakers were known as 'First Publishers of Truth'. Quakers, however, have not tended to make it a group practice as was done in the monasteries, though parts of the *Advices and Queries* are regularly read out at meetings for worship. Instead, they have tended to make it a significant means of private spiritual refreshment.

The art of reading a book slowly and meditatively has to be practised. If we read a book with a spiritual content in the right way, we will be meditating, particularly in the Western sense of the word, which is an active one. When we read normally, we are eager to get to the end, or at least to the next page, to see what else the writer has to say to us. In spiritual reading, it is essential to be aware of the present moment, and not think ahead or even try to remember what has gone before. Remembering will happen automatically if we can relax and be aware, but if we constantly think back, we will lose the sense of 'now' which is so important. There is a need to take frequent pauses, to allow ourselves to be open to what the writer has to say to us personally. Perhaps a word or phrase will leap out at us, and we might take time to ponder this, and discover what this also means for us. If it seems meaningful enough, we might even be prepared to read no further for the time being.

It is no use reading this way if all you want is more knowledge. Spiritual reading is the way of wisdom and understanding, and the way of wisdom is often nonsense to the mind, but joy to the heart. Just as much of the profound teaching we can receive comes to us in silence, so this kind of reading has an undercurrent of silence running through it. We could almost call it 'gathered reading'. Such a way of reading is like visiting a wise teacher. If we have deep questions before we go, we may forget them completely in the presence of the teacher, but find that we have the answers when we get back to our homes. We gain more from the presence of the teacher, which puts us in touch with our own soul, than from struggling to put into words what is essentially beyond thoughts, concepts and ideas. We cannot be open to new ideas if we approach the book knowing the answers – or thinking we do – or even if our minds are so fixed on the questions that we do not pay attention. But even though I am suggesting you avoid such concepts, it is hard to give this advice without falling into the trap of yet another one.

Since many of the early spiritual classics of Quakerism were written in the seventeenth and eighteenth centuries it is important that we read them in the right spirit in order to get their full message. The ordinary way of reading may present barriers of unfamiliar phraseology and sentence length. The method of reading outlined above will help to overcome any barriers of language that might have interfered with our being able to learn from them. Try it – enjoy it – and see for yourselves.

Journal Writing

Do not be afraid to say what you have found and what you value. Appreciate that doubt and questioning can also lead to spiritual growth and to a greater awareness of the Light that is in us all. (5)

The perfect complement to spiritual reading is the spiritual journal. Throughout their history, Quakers have been great journal writers, and some of them are still available to us today. The best known example is probably *The Journal of George Fox*, which still provides Friends with an inspiration which is beyond words. Though the language is of a time far removed from us, there is a power in it that is absolutely timeless. But this is by no means the only one. There are many others. *Quaker Faith and Practice*, the handbook of Britain Yearly Meeting, is full of stunning and inspiring quotes from the journals of Quakers, from our own as well as from the seventeenth and eighteenth centuries.

Journal writing is not just something from the past, and it is not just something that is recommended for a chosen, talented few. It is a private thing, so you can choose how you do it, and no-one will ever read it if you don't want them to. Like the Quaker faith itself, it is there for anyone who feels attracted to it, as well as being a significant spiritual practice in its own right.

But what do we write? The answer is, anything. Journal writing can be an end in itself, or a support to other spiritual practices. It does not always have to be verbal. If you feel you can draw your experience, possibly in cartoon or even abstract form, then this is a useful addition to the words. Poetry, or fragments of poems, are also helpful, whether remembered from other sources or composed for ourselves. Don't be afraid of humour. A few jokes or humorous events lighten the spiritual life in a delightful and helpful way.

Some of the books of instruction on the technique of journaling have a structured outline that can be off-putting unless you feel you need it. If this is to be one of your spiritual practices, it is better to find your own way and discover what is most helpful to you in recording the fruits of your spiritual practice, and in discerning a pattern which might be beneficial in the future. Experiment, for there is really no right or wrong way.

The important thing about journal writing is not to set yourself an impossible goal. You have to bear in mind the amount of time you have available, and the degree to which you feel that you actually want to do it. As with reading, it should be a pleasure. If you feel you can only spare ten minutes a day, then that is the goal you should set yourself. It will do wonders for the brevity of your style and, if you enjoy it, the time will expand itself. The vital thing is to be realistic about what you want from a journal.

Some people just cannot do it. I speak from experience. I have never been able to keep a spiritual journal, though I have often tried. This does not stop me from recognising that it is a good thing to do. I have made a number of starts, with the best intentions, but they have always fizzled out within a few months. I do write an occasional journal, or what I call 'notes to myself' (taken from the title of Hugh Prather's wonderful book – a classic example of modern journal writing, though I don't think he uses the term), and I find this rewarding and refreshing. I also write occasional poems, though I don't show them to anyone.

There are many ways of spiritual writing without keeping a formal journal, and each person must find the way that suits them best. I am fortunate to have a number of spiritual friends from a variety of spiritual pathways. What I enjoy is writing letters to them, and reading their replies, and I manage to do some of this correspondence almost every day.

If you really cannot make the commitment to write for even ten minutes a day and enjoy it, then don't start. It may be that journal writing is not for you, or that you will get the benefits from one of the other forms of writing mentioned above, or from something completely different. If you are not sure, and yet you really feel you *want* to do it, then make a start. You will soon know whether journal writing is for you.

Bible Study

How does Jesus speak to you today? Are you following Jesus' example of love in action? Are you learning from his life the reality and cost of obedience to God? How does his relationship with God challenge and inspire you? [4]

Another significant means of spiritual refreshment which is firmly within the Quaker tradition is that of

Bible study. However, we must recognise that some people have come to Quakerism as an escape from more scripturally-based religion. The Bible has always been important to Friends, but their approach to it is not an orthodox one. The suggestion of Bible study as a means of spiritual refreshment is something that will only appeal to those for whom the Bible still has a meaning, or who want to discover if looking at the Bible through Quaker eyes will make it come alive for them once again. If we decide for ourselves that the Bible – or parts of it, however small – still has a part to play in our spiritual journey, then there are several new ways of study that Quakers have discovered which could be tried.

Any specifically Quaker approach to Bible study should bear in mind the following points:

1. It should apply Quaker insights, understanding and standards, and respect and support the important and specific aspects of the Quaker tradition.
2. It should affirm that of God in all the participants, and thus the equality of all.
3. It should not expect or appoint any authority figure as leader.
4. All present should be able to experience the Spirit working out of the silence.
5. It should emphasise the availability of continuing revelation in our spiritual lives.
6. It should recognise the authority of personal experience as central to our spiritual lives.
7. It should connect the message of the Bible to the conduct of our daily lives.

8. It should affirm the continuing nature of our journeys in a community of faith.[18]

For George Fox and other early Friends, the Bible was a guide which helped them to confirm the experience of God in their lives and worship. It was virtually their sole source of spiritual language, and they quoted it often. Most of us do not have this familiarity, and our study needs to reflect our spiritual journey. There are many ways to study the Bible as a whole, but one of the best that I have discovered is called *Friendly Bible Study*, pioneered by two American Friends, Joanne and Larry Spears. It is designed for groups, and if you wish to practise it in a group, then you will need to obtain a copy of the booklet (*see* Appendix 2) as it contains detailed instruction for the smooth running of such a group study. However, the principles that they outline are so valuable in outlining a specifically Quaker approach to Bible study that I believe they can be applied to individual study as well. In their booklet they liken their approach to a group of blind persons studying an elephant. Each one brings their own perceptions to the consideration of the whole, and each view is accepted as important.

Bearing these points in mind, start by choosing a particular book of the Bible which you want to work with. It might be easier to start with the Gospels of Matthew, Mark or Luke, or one of the letters of Paul. In the Old Testament, you might choose the Psalms or one of the prophets, like Jonah, Amos or Hosea. However, as Quakers have a particular affinity with the Gospel of John, some Friends might want to start there, even though it is one of the more difficult books.

Read a short passage at a time. In a group, each person

will contribute to the ensuing discussion, and the whole will create a picture. On your own, you may have to proceed more slowly, allowing time for silence between each idea that arises. The following five questions, on which the group study is based, provide a framework within which individual as well as group study can flourish. The study questions are:

1. What is the author's main point in this passage? (MAIN POINT)
2. What new light do I find in this particular reading of this passage of the text? (NEW LIGHT)
3. Is this passage true to my experience? (TRUTH)
4. What are the implications of this passage for my life? (IMPLICATIONS)
5. What problems do I have with this passage? (PROBLEMS)[19]

Certain other points can be taken from the group practice, and applied to individual study. In a group, there is no other authority, and people are asked only to bring their Bible and a notebook to the session. Groups are also asked to make a commitment to meet for one hour a week for six weeks. Both of these disciplines might be accepted by an individual, although a reliable commentary and/or a concordance might be of help for someone studying on their own. It is a good idea to keep to the schedule, and not pass judgement on the effectiveness of the study until, say, six sessions have passed.

It is better to undertake to commit one hour a week to this specific practice, rather than trying to do something every day, which is a temptation if you are working on your own. If you have more time to spare on other days, you can contemplate prayerfully what you have learned, rather than trying to cram more and more study each day. As presented here, Bible study is an exercise of spiritual refreshment rather than of learning for its own sake. Of course, mental stimulation is also a part of our lives, and formal study can also be stimulating and refreshing. The two are not mutually exclusive.

Another form of study which I have used, which is itself a meditation, has opened out the Bible to me in ways that I had not thought possible. I was one of those Friends who had escaped – or thought I had – from Judeo-Christian language, and from the Bible. I needed to re-discover the Bible in a Quaker context, and this way of studying, though I did not learn it from a Quaker source, did just that for me.

The first thing is to find a passage which has a meaning for you. Even if you no longer relate to the Bible as a whole, this should not be too difficult. Sit quietly, and read this passage slowly, in a similar way to that outlined in the section on spiritual reading, pondering the meaning of the individual words as well as the passage as a whole. Be aware of a partic-ular word or phrase that might seem to leap out at you. Allow the mind to flow freely around the passage, or the word or phrase, and think of all the possible associations that this may have.

At this stage you might want to have a notebook beside you, and write down any new insights that come to you. Writing is not an essential part of the exercise. It depends whether you are one of those people who likes to have a written record of study, or someone who trusts to memory. Nevertheless, as you are opening yourself out to new inspira-tion, and as this is a study time, not just a meditation, then it is a good idea to have the notebook, even if you decide not to use it.

Allow yourself time to ponder the passage you have chosen, and then pick up your Bible again. This time, open it at random, and select the first short passage that you see. Give this the same treatment, whether or not it is something that at first sight makes sense to you, or even if it is something that causes a reaction. If you persevere with this practice, leaving time for silence between reading, then whole new passages from the Bible will come to have a meaning for you. These last three words are important. Resist the temptation to share your insights with others, until they have become a full part of your life, and you are fully grounded in the practice. If it is right for you to share them, then this will be made clear to you.

What happened to me was that, out of the blue, someone asked me to give a talk on the Bible. I was quite well known for speaking to various groups, and had been teaching work-shops on meditation, Buddhism and comparative religion for some time but no-one – as far as I knew – associated me with the Bible. Nonetheless, because I had studied in this way for several months before the request came, the talk went very well, and I was later asked back to give another one.

Spiritual Healing

Are you open to the healing power of God's love? [2] ...
Hold yourself and others in the Light, knowing that all
are cherished by God. [3]

From the time of Jesus, there has always been a healing ministry within the Christian church, and this was one of the Gifts of the Spirit that early Friends re-discovered. There are also records of healing miracles in the Jewish faith, in ancient Egypt, in India and in every country in the world where there is a written religious history. Though healing continued to be important in the early church, the story since that time – with a few exceptions – is one of steady decline until relatively modern times. This coincided with the rise of medical healing.

From the accounts in the Gospels, we can get some idea of the range and power of Jesus's healing ministry. He was quite clear that his healing was the other half of his ministry. He instructed his disciples to heal the sick and preach the Gospel. Whether it was because the second part was easier, or the first part needed a greater discipline than his followers were prepared to attempt, the preaching gained ascendancy over the healing. Or perhaps, as has been suggested, it was because of the increasing deification of Jesus. If Jesus was the only Son of God, then regardless of what he had asked us to do, we could not hope to follow his example. Whatever the reason, the healing ministry only arose through a few saintly individuals and, with the increasing power of the church, it became dangerous for those not in holy orders to claim to heal the sick by prayer. They might – and many did – get tried for witchcraft.

George Fox had powerful gifts of healing and prayer, and there are a number of outstanding examples recorded in his *Journal*. In fact, he was accused of being a witch several times. He wrote a manuscript entitled *The Book of Miracles* which, along with his other writings, he requested should be published after his death. Possibly because the climate had changed, and the idea of healing miracles was not respectable, this was not done. However, the existence of the manuscript was sufficiently well known for extracts from it to appear in the manuscript *Annual Catalogue* of Fox's papers which appeared after his death. From these and other sources, the Quaker historian Henry J Cadbury assembled a reconstruction of the *Book of Miracles* which was published in 1948, and which lists over one hundred and fifty healing miracles attributed to Fox.[20]

Spiritual healing and intercessory prayer have a very important place in Quaker practice. Because early Friends saw themselves as reviving primitive Christianity, and because they were sure that the Christ within was a living reality, they were open to the ministry of healing. Encouraged by this, and by the instructions of Jesus to pray for one another, many Quakers today try to give some time each day to thinking of those who are sick or otherwise in need of prayer.

As we open ourselves to become a channel of God's healing grace we shall find that healing is given to those who pray as well as to those for whom we are praying.
(Jack Dobbs, QFP, 21.73)

The most common form of healing prayer among Friends is the practice of 'holding someone in the

Light'. There are two main ways of doing this. If we know the person, we can actually visualise them enfolded by the Light of God's Love. We can see this Light permeating every aspect of their being, and filling any dark patches which might be seen as disease. If we do not know them well enough for this, we can meditate on the Light itself, knowing that the light that is within us is also within them, and accepting that God's will for them is being fulfilled. In fact, we have discovered that almost any form of meditation on the Divine and Its qualities, on God and his Love or any similar approach will bring healing to those who are remembered in this way.

This is only one of the practices that Friends who are involved in the healing ministry use. There is in Britain a Friends Fellowship of Healing who publish a wide range of literature on the subject. Some Friends also practice personal healing on a one-to-one basis. In this, they may use the technique of laying on of hands – either on the head or on the point of pain – which has been traditional in the Christian Church since the time of Jesus, or they may sit quietly and just worship, pray or meditate with someone.

The important thing to remember at all times is that we do not do the healing. Furthermore, we do not of ourselves know how to, or even what to pray for. While there are some Friends – particularly among Quakers in Africa and the USA – for whom inspired vocal prayer is a vital part of their healing process, this is used to help surrender the one needing prayer to the Love of God. It is not for the purpose of telling God what to do for a particular person.

In the many years I have been practising spiritual healing – and I discovered this before I came to the Quakers – I have been made aware that I too gain blessings from praying for others. It is as if I am included in my own prayers, whether or not I seek it. Another thing is that it helps me to remember my daily prayer and meditation. If I was doing it solely for myself, I might easily forget, but if I have the responsibility of praying for others, it is easier to remember. So are we blessed by giving blessings.

Worshipping Alone

For Quakers, the whole idea of meeting for worship is a group activity. Yet, as the *Advices* remind us, we can worship alone. If for some reason we need to do so, we have to make a definite intention. Because worship is traditionally a group activity, there is a powerful inner barrier to overcome. It is helpful to remember that in the Quaker tradition we are not alone when we settle down to worship. There are stories about meetings which have diminished in size until only one elderly Friend is left, and that Friend faithfully unlocks the meeting house and sits in the silence every Sunday morning. Yet the stories emphasise that she is not alone. Christ – or God if you prefer – the unseen Friend is always there when we worship. And, from this faithfulness, others have been attracted in a marvellous and unsought manner until the meeting is thriving again. As the old saying goes, 'One, with God, is a majority'.

When we realise the Presence of God, we do not have to tell anyone. Even if we sit down in the middle of the city or the desert, we will discover that those people who are our true spiritual friends will find us. This has been the Quaker experience, both in the stories mentioned above, and also with Friends who have moved to an area where there was no meeting, and who have faithfully sat and worshipped alone on a regular basis. They have soon found their spiritual Friends.

Once we have overcome the inner barrier to worshipping alone, then the procedure is exactly the same as in a local meeting. We sit and wait, with the intention of knowing the reality of God within us. We may make an arrangement with one or more people that we will all sit at the same time, and then as we centre down to be with them in spirit, it will feel as if we are with them physically. Even if we are unable to contact other Friends, we are not alone. We can be sure that somewhere in the world there is someone else who is praying, meditating or worshipping in words, music or silence. And if that person is a member of our spiritual family – and God alone knows this – we will be united with them in the living silence.

When worshipping or meditating alone, I have occasionally felt the need to go to a specific book and read a passage. It seems as though this is a substitute for ministry, to provide inspiration and direction for my contemplation. Even in a normal meeting, some Friend may feel the urge to go to the table and take the Bible or *Quaker Faith and Practice*, and either read a passage out loud, or speak based on what they have been inspired to read.

However, although I believe that we can worship alone, there are definite differences. There is the testimony of the senses, particularly those of sight and hearing, and the value and inspiration of ministry. Then there is the feeling of being part of a congregation, a community, which has been one of the integral parts of Christianity from the beginning. Such a feeling does not have to include the physical presence of others, but we have to use our imagination more when we are on our own. However, creative imagination is by no means a bad tool to have on our spiritual journey.

I should also add that there are Friends who disagree with me, and say that the power of meeting with others is essential in Quaker practice. I can only write of my experience of the times when, for one reason or another, I have had to – or even wanted to – worship alone. For me, the only essential difference lies in the companionship that is there when the meeting is over, and if I was feeling solitary and did not want company, then that was all right too.

So what is the difference between worship on one's own and the contemplative meditation described at the beginning of this chapter? None at all, really; it just shows that spiritual practice goes round in a circle, and we very often finish up where we started, except that we may give it a different name.

Music and the Arts

Along the paths of the imagination the artist and the mystic make contact. The revelations of God are not all of one kind. Always the search in art, as in religion, is for the rhythms of relationships, for the unity, the urge, the wonder of life that is presented in great art and true religion.
(Horace B Pointing, QFP, 21.32)

Early Friends were not interested in music and the arts. In fact, they actively discouraged them as practices in the spiritual life, and saw them as hindrances. In his *Journal*, George Fox said that he was ' ... moved to cry out against all sorts of music ... [for it] burdened the pure life, and stirred peoples minds to vanity.' In the world that they lived in, they may have been right, though some did go to extremes, such as Solomon Eccles, a professional musician who tried to publicly burn his instruments when he became a Quaker. I suspect their experience of music as an aid to worship must have been very limited. Quakers are not alone in this, for throughout history, there have been people who have found the same thing.

Others have found the opposite to be true. They have discovered that music, colour and drama have enhanced their spiritual practice. Examples can be found in Hindu temples, where the extravagances of carving, music and dancing have often been misunderstood. In the Orthodox church, there is the famous example of the colour and beauty of the liturgy at the cathedral of Constantinopol, which led the ambassadors of the Tsar of Russia to report that they had discovered the nearest thing to heaven on earth. Their report led to the Orthodox faith becoming the official church in Russia. And in Buddhism, where examples range from the colourful thankas of the Tibetan tradition to the austere black calligraphy of Zen, the arts are accepted as a valid spiritual practice on their own.

Modern Friends have learned to value the arts, but it took them until the latter half of this century to accept music. They have learned from other traditions how valuable music can be as an aid to spiritual practice. In Britain, there is a Quaker Fellowship of the Arts, as well as a Quaker orchestra and chorus which meets occasionally to rehearse performances. Quakers have also recognised the value of music in projecting their Peace Testimony. One of the most famous examples was *The Gates of Greenham*, which had several performances at the Royal Festival Hall in London, and which told the story of the Greenham Common peace protests to a much wider audience.

There are Friends who are writers, poets, painters, singers, dancers, sculptors, calligraphers and flower arrangers, to name but a few. There are Quaker woodturners, potters, furniture makers, and a whole range of craftsmen and women. And, of course, there are those who listen, read, admire and use the things of beauty that they produce.

There is a story that one of the most famous players of the Chinese zither had a friend who was known throughout China as the most famous listener. It is said that when the friend died, the player cut his strings and refused to play again. Quakers can identify with this, such is the value that we place on listening, or on any form of total appreciation.

Retreats

Traditionally, Quakers have been so concerned with the identification of the spiritual life with the everyday that they did not take special times to go on retreat. However, that was when the world was a quieter and less frantic place. Contemporary Friends, who tend increasingly to work for bodies outside the Quaker field, have been quick to recognise that their lives sometimes need that special quiet time away from the daily pressures.

In some ways, retreats come easy to those who are used to worshipping in silence. Naturally, a retreat based on Quaker principles will probably be based on silence, but this will be balanced with times of communication, sharing and space for people to be alone. The 'leader' will be aware that he or she is only a facilitator, and will try not to intrude into the individual's space. Worship will probably not be led in any way, but will be in the Quaker tradition.

There may well be times of led meditation, which will encourage relaxation and visualisation, though these are not specifically Quaker practices. In fact the retreat may draw on many practices from outside the Quaker tradition, and will depend very much on the knowledge, skill and intuition of the leader. Because there is no traditional form for a 'Quaker retreat', they will vary, but there are many Friends whose ministry in this area is becoming increasingly valued.

COMMITMENT

Live adventurously. When choices arise, do you take the
way that offers the fullest opportunity for the use of your
gifts in the service of God and the community? Let your
life speak. [27]

Important though the Meeting for Worship and our personal development might be, they are by no means the
whole of the Quaker way of life. One of the first things that
appealed to me about Quakers was that they do not make a
distinction between the sacred and the secular. Everyday life
is holy. On my office wall is a card with this quotation from
Rabbi Abraham J Herschel of the Jewish Peace Fellowship:

SHALOM; just to be is a blessing, just to live is holy. [21]

Though from the Jewish Hassidic tradition, it could easily have
come from a Quaker, for it expresses the Quaker attitude. The
meeting for worship allows us to know that God is present.

91

The influence of that quiet time together, if we let it, permeates the daily business of earning a living, keeping a home and relating to other people. It is essentially practical. In the silence, the presence of God is realised, but we would agree with Brother Lawrence (the Carmelite lay-brother who was a contemporary of George Fox and the author of the Christian mystical classic *The Practice of the Presence of God*[22]) that this presence can be as real or even more so in the kitchen as in the chapel.

By now you will realise that Quakers feel we can find this Presence, and listen to Its Still Small Voice, whenever we take the time to be still and adopt a listening attitude. The Kingdom of Heaven is within us, but it is incomplete if we do not follow our inspiration towards bringing it to earth. The words of the Lord's Prayer, 'Thy Kingdom come on earth, as it is in Heaven', are an essential part of living the Christian Life as Quakers see it.

Buddhists have an unusual way of pointing to this truth. They say that Nirvana (enlightenment) and samsara (this world) are one. This is similar to Jesus' saying, 'I and my Father are one.' The Zen tradition of Buddhism elaborates with this little story:

> When we first embark on the path, mountains are mountains and trees are trees. When we are farther along, mountains are no longer mountains and trees no longer trees. But when we are fully enlightened, mountains are mountains and trees are trees.[23]

This is an outline of the spiritual life. When we commence, this world is the only reality. Farther along the path, and this world seems unreal. But further still, this world and the 'Kingdom of Heaven' are One.

Early Friends placed a great emphasis on 'Living faithfully', and this is still true today. To live faithfully means that we are true to our own selves, and to the highest and best that we can find within us. This is simple to say, but by no means easy to do. We are all aware of times when we feel that we should take a course of action, but are afraid that it will, for example, make us look foolish to other people. This sort of difficulty can arise many times in the course of an average week. Sometimes we listen, and sometimes we ignore our inner voice.

Sometimes the matter is trivial, and will not affect anyone but ourselves. Sometimes it is more serious, and occasionally it is a life-changing decision. It is human nature to prioritise, and to quickly forget the small occasions. But in fact, these are the training ground, and even here we can learn to draw on help. Help is always there. It is what the religions of the world have called grace, and what George Fox called 'The Power of the Lord'. It enables us to hold firm, and then, as Shakespeare said, we will not be false to others.

———◆———

True godliness don't turn men out of the world, but enables them to live better in it, and excites their endeavours
to mend it. (William Penn)

What is it like to be a Quaker in everyday life. What makes a person a Quaker? We often say that there are more 'natural Quakers' outside the Society of Friends than inside it. Quakerism is often referred to as a way of life rather than a religion, although True Religion – or True Godliness as William Penn calls it – should actually be just that; a way of life.

I like to think of the Quakerness of a person as being like the drone of a sitar or bagpipes; always there and undergirding every tune that is played. Of course, not every tune is suitable for the sitar or bagpipes, and not every musician manages to play the right balance of the drone note and the melody. And the contrast of the drone and the melody is not always comfortable. Similarly, while our Quakerness is always there, we do not always live in harmony with it. We sometimes try to do things that are inappropriate, or try to break free of the limitations that are an inevitable complement to the joys of the Quaker way of life.

Friends are best known to the rest of the world by their 'testimonies', that is, public statements of the principles that they have discovered throughout their history. The testimonies are the first thing that many people know about the Quakers. The best known one is the Peace Testimony, which has brought many people into the Society of Friends, though often it is not fully understood. It is, of course, only one of many. Testimonies are a way of living that grows out of inspiration and the efforts to live up to it in everyday life.

Quaker testimonies have evolved from the specific spiritual insights of individual Friends, as a response to perceived needs. They are usually tested by different groups of Friends before being acted upon. When an individual Friend, or a meeting, observes a need, and receives a specific spiritual impulse to do something about it, this is known as a 'concern'. These concerns are tested in meeting for worship by waiting in silence until it is clear that this is a real leading of the Spirit. If a Meeting decides to uphold the concern, it may do so as a whole, or support an individual or a group of Friends in their actions. If the concern is to become a testimony adopted by the whole Society, it may have to be tested in this way by many groups of Friends, before eventually coming to the annual gathering, where it can be considered by as many as a thousand Quakers. If the concern is real, then the Spirit will guide those involved through every stage of the testing process.

Quaker testimonies do not claim to be unique. There are many people who care about living in harmony with their deepest convictions. For example, Buddhists have the same attitude as part of their Noble Eightfold Path. Quaker testimonies have evolved and changed in response to the needs of each period of history, right up to the present day. Many of the resulting concerns have been taken up by others, who have much greater resources than Friends, so they are more easily able to put them into action. And Friends are happy that this should be so.

Testimonies such as non-violence, simplicity and honesty have been with us from the very beginnings of Quakerism. Some adopted by early Friends (e.g. against the payment of tithes) are no longer relevant, while others, like the recent one adopted by Friends in Britain on homelessness and the lack of housing, have arisen in response to contemporary needs.

———◆◆◆———

Stand firm in our testimony, even when others commit or prepare to commit acts of violence, yet always remember that they too are children of God. [31]

As stated above, the best known testimony of Friends is that to non-violence, known as the Peace Testimony. This is not just an opposition to wars, violence and armaments. When George Fox was offered a captaincy in the army, he told the Commonwealth Commissioners that he ' ... lived in the virtue of that life and power that took away the occasion of all wars.' He added that he ' ... was come into the covenant of peace which was before wars and strife were.' He was not understood, and was put into a ' ... stinking low place in the ground without any bed,'[24] and kept there for almost six months. Through all this, he was able to maintain that inner peace within himself which enabled him not only to survive, but not to seek to escape on the occasions that he was let out to walk in the garden. From this attitude, he won the grudging respect of the gaolers and other inmates of the prison. This is important when considering Quaker attitudes to war.

The history of the written Peace Testimony stems from a declaration to King Charles II in 1660. Friends' position was that of a people who had moved beyond the need to fight for power (because for them the Power of the Lord was the ultimate) or freedom (because in their hearts they were always free in the Power of Christ):

> All bloody principles and practices we do utterly deny, with all outward wars, and strife, and fightings with outward weapons, for any end, or for any pretence whatsoever, and this is our testimony to the whole world. That Spirit of Christ by which we are guided is not changeable, so as once to command us from a thing as evil, and again to move into it; and we do certainly know,

and so testify to the world, that the spirit of Christ which leads us into all truth will never move us to fight and war against any man with outward weapons, neither for the kingdom of Christ, nor for the kingdoms of this world. [25]

Isaac Penington, another early Friend, was even clearer about the fact that the Peace Testimony was not just a condemnation of war. Writing in 1661, he says:

I speak not against any magistrates or peoples defending themselves against foreign invasions, or making use of the sword to suppress the violent and evil-doers within their borders – for this the present state of things may and doth require ... yet there is a better state which the Lord hath already brought some into, and which the nations are to expect and travel towards. There is to be a time when 'nation shall not lift up sword against nation, neither shall they learn war any more' ... This blessed state, which shall be brought forth [in society] at large in God's season, must begin in particulars [that is, individuals]. [26]

Contemporary Friends express it another way:

We may disagree with the views of the politician or the soldier who opts for a military solution, but we still respect and cherish the person. [27]

As repeated statements will show, Quakers have expressed this opposition to war and 'fighting with outward weapons' for over three hundred years. This has led most Friends to be conscientious objectors when it came to being called up into the armed forces. Even here, the primacy of the individual's inner guidance is clearly seen. Some Quakers fought, believing there was no other way, while for others being a conscientious objector meant going to prison as the ultimate statement of the Quaker testimony against war. Yet others worked on the land, in hospitals, or in some other occupation which they saw as constructive as opposed to the destructive business of war.

Quakers themselves took positive steps to show their opposition to the forced drafting of civilians. They founded organisations such as the Friends Ambulance Unit and the Friends Relief Service to provide positive relief from the suffering caused by war. The FAU was founded in 1915, and worked throughout the First World War in hospitals and in education and welfare. They also served in France and Belgium, and on hospital ships. Though not an official part of the Society of Friends, it was supported by the Yearly Meeting and by many Quaker firms and individuals.

When the Second World War stared in 1939, the FAU was revived. By the end of the war, members had seen service in twenty-five different countries in Europe, Africa, the Middle East and Asia, and had contributed to the welfare and relief work for many thousands of its casualties. As with the earlier group, not all the members were Quakers, and this time most of them were in their twenties. Their work took them to some of the most difficult and dangerous parts of the war, and they often came into conflict with the military authorities, and occasionally with the Yearly Meeting at home. They maintained their civilian status at all times, and served – as far as they were allowed to – all those in need, regardless of nationality or creed.

The Friends Relief Service was founded in the early 1940s (though it functioned under several different names). Its purpose was the relief of civilian suffering, and at first it worked almost entirely in Britain. Its members were not all Quakers – indeed, some were not even pacifists – but they were all people who cared deeply about the suffering of the innocent victims of war. They did welfare work in air-raid shelters and rest centres, worked in clubs, settlements, advice centres and hostels for evacuees and those who had lost their homes. They did their best to respond wherever there was a need.

These organisations were very different, but are typical examples of the way in which those Friends who heard the urgings of the Spirit translated it into practice. Since their founding, Quakers have become known for responding to the sufferings of the world in a practical way. Being a relatively small group, we cannot just respond to every need, but rather choose those to which we feel guided. This applies equally to individual Friends, as well as Quakers as a community.

Search out whatever in your own way of life may contain the seeds of war. [31]

This is not the whole story. As with George Fox, the aim of the Quaker Life is to give people that state of inner peace where war, violence and injustice cannot exist. This was the power Jesus spoke of when he said 'My peace I *give* you; not as the world giveth … ' (*emphasis mine*). This attitude is relevant in everyday life. We are reminded of the need to continually be aware of the violence that is around us, and our own violent reactions to the world we live it. James Nayler, an ecstatic and visionary seventeenth-century Friend who, with some of his disciples, acted out the triumphant entry of Jesus into Jerusalem and was horribly tortured and branded as a blasphemer, discovered this peace in the end. Just before he died he wrote the beautiful and often quoted passage which exemplifies the essence of the Quaker Peace Testimony, and indeed all the testimonies of Friends:

> There is a Spirit which I feel that delights to do no evil, nor to revenge any wrong, but delights to endure all things, in hope to enjoy its own in the end. Its hope is to outlive all wrath and contention, and to weary out all exaltation and cruelty, or whatever is a nature contrary to itself. [28]

How could anyone write something as beautiful as this after enduring horrendous sufferings, unless inspired by something greater that themselves?

'There is a spirit which I feel … ' First comes the affirmation that there *is* something that is beyond our own abilities, which we can come to feel, and this feeling can enable us to act in a way that might not be possible to our ordinary human natures. Whether or not we wish to call it God, it is a reality that has been discovered by Quakers and others which provides power when we are powerless. Even if we think that our human nature is enough for our present life, then we can call it Love, and if we acknowledge that Love is greater than our human will, then Love will empower us to do things that we never thought possible. We have to find that spirit in some way or another.

Next comes the declaration that this Spirit wishes no harm to anyone; that it is the spirit of unconditional Love. Remember, this was written just before Nayler died, and after he had been through the most dreadful persecution for nothing more than an ecstatic vision of his unity with Christ. Nayler has been little understood, even by Quakers who disowned him for a time, but anyone with a knowledge of ecstatic religion in, say, India, will recognise the state in which the devotee gains union with the form of the God which he or she worships. Sad to say, seventeenth-century England did not have this clarity of vision. However, out of it all came one of the most beautiful affirmations of peace in the English language.

Here again we see that one clear way to achieve this contact with God is to develop the art of inner listening. This practice is strengthened by coming together with others. It is further strengthened if we are aware of it in small things, so that we can see the way in which the Spirit works in and with us. There is neither great nor small in the Kingdom of Heaven. Early Friends were often called to make great sacrifices, and as we only have their writings to go on, it is not always clear how the spirit was leading them. Many others throughout history have also found this way of living, and have also testified to its benefits. The extra dimension that Quakers have offered is the way in which groups can test the leadings to be sure that they are genuinely inspired.

This exercise of testing concerns has been a part of Quaker practice from the very beginning. It requires that we have a degree of trust that we may find that we are completely wrong, partly misled or even right (which can take as much trust and courage as either of the other possibilities). We have to be prepared to trust those who are meeting with us to try to discern what is right, and we have to trust the movement of the Spirit among us to be able to show us the way forward.

This trust is helped by the Quaker way of reaching decisions, which is discussed in detail in the next chapter. The Quaker 'meeting for worship for business' places us in a situation where we can turn to the Spirit for guidance, confirmation and empowerment. In order that this can work skilfully, the person who brings the concern to be tested is a part of the group, and is as concerned to find the will of God as any other member. They are not on trial, and neither are their ideas. Whether the idea goes forward will not be the result of a majority decision, and neither can the meeting be 'packed' with opponents of the idea. The spirit of worship will prevail, and there will be a member appointed as clerk to guide the process of consideration, and at least one or more elders to see that the spirit of worship is maintained.

Truth and Honesty

Our responsibilities to God and our neighbour may involve us in taking unpopular stands. [38]

While the Peace Testimony is probably the best known Quaker testimony, there are many others. Early Friends were known for their honesty and truthfulness.

In this, they followed the teaching of Jesus, 'Let your communication be yea, yea; nay, nay; for whatsoever is more than these cometh of evil,'[29] and the example of George Fox.

This testimony to truth and honesty in all that we say and do was the guiding principle that led Friends to object to swearing oaths in court. They maintained that one should be truthful at all times, and refused to allow a court appearance to be anything special. This eventually led to Quakers being allowed to affirm in court, rather than formally promising to tell the truth while invoking God and with their hands on the Bible. This has also had repercussions for other faith groups, who, for one reason or another, are unable to use the official form of oath. For instance, Buddhists, for whom the existence of God is not an important part of their faith, can also find difficulty with the formal wording.

In the seventeenth century, all non-conformists were barred from universities and the professions. As a result of this, many Friends were involved in trading or retail businesses. Their testimony to Truth soon became known, and their businesses prospered. Dealing with Friends was a straightforward matter. They did not encourage bargaining, and if they asked a price, it was always fair, but was usually fixed (unless they could be persuaded that they were being unfair). They saw being willing to reduce prices under pressure as dishonest. Today, with many Friends in the caring professions, this attitude is extended towards their clients, who soon come to know that being a Quaker means that yes is yes and no, no. But it does not mean that Quakers are inflexible. Listening to what people are actually saying means that we are able to change as circumstances demand, but that we treat people honestly and expect them to do the same in their dealings with us.

Simplicity

———◆◆◆———

Try to live simply. A simple lifestyle freely chosen is a source of strength. (41)

Quakers have long had a testimony towards simplicity in living. Today, this leads them to be concerned about waste, about the environment, and about the sharing of world resources. As with other aspects of the Quaker way of life, each person must find their own ways of expression. Some will feel it right to limit the things that they possess to the absolute minimum, while others will apply the test as to whether any object has a use. Each person discovers their own areas of difficulty. Most Friends that I know who find it relatively easy to live simply in other ways, still have difficulty over the question of books – particularly Quaker books – and possess large libraries. The Quaker way does not propose rules, but encourages us to be aware, and work out the right solution for ourselves.

We do not own the world, nor do we have the right to exploit it, or to exploit other beings who share it with us. For some Friends, this means being a vegetarian – or vegan – and opposing experiments on animals for any reason whatsoever. Most would oppose the use of animals for cosmetic research, and some for medical research. These feel that what is morally wrong will not be scientifically right in the end.

Quakers are also concerned about the exploitation of the natural resources of our planet, and some are active in organisations such as Greenpeace or Friends of the Earth. They oppose the use of nuclear power, as this has links with the armaments industry, but also because of the toxic waste that it creates.

Quakers share with Buddhists the idea of 'Right Livelihood' (the Buddhist term). In earlier times, because Friends were prevented from attending university, they were mostly found in trade and industry. Even there, there was a concern that money made should be used rightfully, and Quaker firms tended to be caring of their workers. In the UK the Quaker chocolate firms of Cadbury and Rowntree both had a deep concern for housing, firstly for their workers, and then on a wider scale. Today, Friends tend to move towards the caring professions and teaching.

As we have seen, in earlier times Friends were opposed to the arts, feeling that they distracted people from the essential elements of the spiritual life and from the simplicity of living, which was one of the Quaker ideals. Today, though Friends still have a testimony to simple living, they accept that the arts have an important place within this, and can add significantly to the richness and joy of life. Quakers may be found taking part in most aspects of artistic expression, and some even find employment in this field.

In this, as in all that they do, Friends try to be guided by the Spirit. We do have a tendency to see something wrong, and immediately want to do something about it. However, we realise that as a relatively small religious organisation, with limited resources, we cannot put right all the world's wrongs. That is why we support other organisations – some of which have grown out of Quaker concerns – which have the resources and contacts. In the Society of Friends today, there are very few members who are not active in giving some of their time and resources to one or more of the many organisations working towards making this world a better place to live in, and bringing the kingdom of Heaven to earth.

Equality

———◆———

Bring into God's Light those emotions, attitudes and prejudices in yourself which lie at the root of destructive conflict, acknowledging your need for forgiveness and grace. [32]

There are two other testimonies that are of particular significance to daily life in the modern world. The first is the recognition of equality in all people regardless of colour, sex, religion, sexual orientation, politics or any other differences of birth, belief or practice. The second is the complement to it; that of being non-judgmental and listening to what people say without bias. Both of these are attitudes that have to be learned, but they arise out of the movement of the Spirit.

We all have, whether we have ever faced them or not, some prejudices. These may have arisen from our own personal experiences. For example, the only people of a specific skin colour that we have come across may have been those who have bullied, attacked or abused us or other people around us. The same may apply to people of a different religion or social class. We automatically associate by reaction people of a similar colour or class – whoever they are – with an attack situation. But it still creates prejudice. If we can become aware of our reactions, we will have taken the first step in removing prejudice, and also in harmonising our contacts with such people.

The Quaker idea of 'that of God' within all people is a great help in this. If we can train ourselves to recognise the latent Divine Spirit within another person, a different response will arise within us when we are faced with them. This in turn has an effect on them. In these days of popular psychology, we all know a little about body language. Body language is an unconscious expression of our thoughts and feelings, and if they are bent on recognising the Divine everywhere, and particularly in the person to whom we have a reaction, then our body language will convey a different message from that which would otherwise be the case.

Quakers have long been in the forefront of seeking to understand homosexuality. In 1963 Friends felt a concern for this and other matters of sexuality. After much testing, they published a report by a group of Friends with special understanding in these matters. *Towards a Quaker View of Sex*, as the booklet was called, created a furore. It was the first time that any Christian body had openly addressed these issues, and it won Quakers new friends and new enemies. The booklet was revised and went through a number of editions. In the same year, they also published *Homosexuality from the Inside* by David Blamires, a gay Friend who felt able to be open about his sexuality. This led to the setting up of a Quaker Gay and Lesbian Fellowship to provide a space where gay and lesbian Friends could meet and discuss matters relating to their spirituality and sexuality. This Fellowship still exists, and has published a number of books of its own.

Quakers are encouraged to, 'Hold yourself and others in the Light, knowing that all are cherished by God'.[3] This practice was discussed in detail in the section on spiritual healing, and reminds us that Jesus told us not only to love our neighbours – which includes our enemies – but to love them as ourselves. It is so easy to forget this last part. We have been conditioned to think that loving ourselves is selfish, but it is not. Truly loving ourselves is an essential part of loving others. Many Friends make this or something similar a part of their daily practice.

In the early days, Friends were often able to transform the attitude of magistrates and prison guards by their attitude of not physically resisting evil. This ideal of passive resistance was most effectively used by Gandhi in this century, when he persuaded many of his followers not to react when they were attacked, beaten or even fired upon. In the last instance, our lives are seen as being of less importance than the testimony against violence. This belief requires a great deal of what Gandhi called 'Soul-power', or an inner conviction that the Power of the Spirit is able to prevail.

This ideal has not worked on every occasion that it has been tried, yet there have been enough occasions where it has for those who believe in it to appreciate its significance, and be inspired by it. In the Americas, Quakers were able to relate to the Indian tribes through this inner peace, which was demonstrated outwardly by their not locking doors, not owning guns and other weapons – except perhaps for hunting – and their meeting in silence without any of the furious preaching which typified other Europeans.

Creative Listening

Creative Listening developed out of the realisation that a person cannot give full attention to what is being said to them at the same time as assessing it and framing a reply. I cannot do this, and neither can anyone else I have ever met. Therefore, true listening rarely occurs.
(Rachel Pinney, *Creative Listening*)

When we begin to see that there is that of God within all beings, then we automatically value them for themselves. We learn to listen without judgement to what they may have to say. It is not an exaggeration to state that to listen to someone with your total attention can be a transforming experience for both parties. Quakers have been known for this from the beginning, and have often been used to negotiate a truce between warring parties. Though early Friends could be quite vocal in their opposition to those things that they felt were wrong, the strength of their arguments was increased because they had listened carefully and openly to those of their opponents. However, they also listened to and obeyed the Inner Voice which required them to 'Judge not' and 'Resist not evil', and was the final authority.

This ability has to be learned, and re-learned by every generation in order to relate to the world in which it is practised. One very successful technique which helps is that of Creative Listening, which was founded in 1960 by Dr Rachel Pinney, a Quaker and medical doctor. In her booklet, *Creative Listening*, she says: 'This method is very specific, and requires close attention and the *learned ability to switch off the demanding self.*'[30] (my emphasis)

In order to fully convey the transforming nature of this experience I cannot do better than quote from *Creative Listening*. In summing up the problem, Rachel Pinney says:

> When two people meet to discuss *one* subject, what usually happens is that they really discuss *two* subjects, the two viewpoints that each one is putting forward. If full understanding is to take place only one subject, that is one person's viewpoint, should be considered at any one time.
>
> I do not believe that total listening can be achieved by an act of will alone. A person who decides to listen by making an act of will inevitably gives some attention to the act of will. In using the Creative Listening method the act of will is made at the start, before the 'listen' takes place.
>
> Having made this initial decision, it is possible completely to listen to another person by consciously adopting some very simple techniques. With practice, these enable almost everyone to achieve 'single attention', whatever the views of the speaker and however great the urge to interrupt would otherwise be. Basically, the method consists of the listener *totally switching off his or her own views for the duration of the*

'listen'. By doing so he is able to give his total attention to the speaker. In the process, he or she will have a brand-new experience: by not interrupting or arguing he will hear things that he has never heard before.

The speaker, too, will have a brand-new experience. He will be aware that he is being heard by someone who is not going to come back at him with a reply, criticism or opposition. And not only is he heard, he hears himself. This is a fantastic experience, and it sends the speaker away re-thinking the subject, often for weeks to come.

What about the listener's desire to answer back? It is my experience that when one side of a controversy is fully heard, *there is no need for the other side to be heard*. One act of listening to one side of a controversy causes people to re-think their views. [31] (author's emphasis)

She goes on to say that the only way to achieve all this is through practice. It is my experience that once the basic principle has been grasped, it is easy to work out a method to suit whatever circumstances are prevailing. One thing that is important to remember is that no-one should be pressurised to speak. Some of us want to be silent in such circumstances, and it is no bad thing for two or more people to come naturally to a shared silence.

Creative listening has an obvious relationship to the Peace Testimony in that it is of practical help in resolving conflicts. It also expresses a principle that we can apply in our everyday lives, and not just in the special circumstances of conflict resolution. If you are aware and listening, you will be amazed how many opportunities arise for you to listen to others with the whole of your being, which is what this technique is teaching us to do. And when you listen in this way, it is as if there is another Presence with you, bringing another dimension to the practice.

The Inner Voice

Quakers and many others who are practised in prayer and meditation have had the experience of an insistent inner voice which moves them towards a specific course of action. In the silence this voice is at first soft and gentle, but if it is not heeded it can become stronger and stronger until the course of action is clear. Quakers call this a 'concern', and it is this which is the source of many of the testimonies that are later adopted by the whole of the Quaker family.

This word concern is not used in the sense of 'concern about something' but rather it is a clear understanding that some task has been 'inwardly laid upon me by God'. Traditionally, with Quakers' Christian heritage, this means acceptance of a personal God. However, today there are an increasing number of Friends who do not accept a personal God, yet their experience with the impersonal Spirit in the silence is the same. They are still able to point to the experience of an inner leading, and a feeling of being in harmony with the universe when they follow it.

We noted earlier that Friends have ways of testing these concerns, and that it is this testing which establishes whether or not they are genuine. In order to fully understand the degree to which concerns are considered, it is necessary to have some knowledge of the structure of the Society of Friends. I will use the example of Britain Yearly Meeting, though Friends in other countries have different but similar structures. The local worshipping group is called a Preparative Meeting, so-called because it prepares Friends for the Monthly Meeting (a group of PMs which manage property, decide membership matters and look at concerns). A group of MMs is called a General Meeting (formerly a Quarterly Meeting).

At a national level (in the UK), there is Meeting for Sufferings, which is the main executive body of British Friends. This was originally founded in the seventeenth century to deal with the sufferings of Quakers who were being persecuted for their beliefs, and has retained its original name. Finally, there is the Yearly Meeting, which is the final authority on matters that are to be taken up by the Society as a whole. There are also numerous other committees which exist for specific purposes.

From this description it will be apparent that a Friend who has a concern must be very sure and determined to get it all the way through to consideration at a national level. A Friend who feels a concern is being laid upon them by God will hold it for a while, to see if it stays, and even if it grows in its intensity. They may ask an informal group to meet with them and pray about it. If it is felt to be genuine, then it will be brought to the local Meeting, the Monthly Meeting and sometimes the General Meeting. Any of these meetings may appoint a group of Friends to meet with the concerned Friend to consider the matter further. Such groups have the advantage of time, in that they have no other matter to consider. Only after all this will the concern, supported by minutes, be passed up to Meeting for Sufferings.

An outstanding example of this process was the concern that came to a Friend called George Murphy for the establishment of a Chair of Peace Studies at a British university. It started with a number of significant meetings for worship, and came to a head when, in the village of Grantchester near Cambridge, came the clear inner message, '*You* shall do it, and *I* shall help'.[32] Although some Friends were hesitant, feeling that this was excessively emotional, others were deeply moved.

His account continues:

> But note, I never intended to leave Manchester University to go to Bradford. Once there, look how fast every door was opened! When all was settled – money, the Chair established, and all that was required as Robert McKinley said ' ... and where is the man or woman coming from to fill such a Chair?' My reply was, 'I do not know', but later when Adam Curle came on the scene Robert said, 'If ever there was a case of divine providence!' So how can I explain in the written word why the concern went to such an undreamed-of success? I have since travelled the world, as you know, but still Bradford is to the forefront: it has NO equal in skill, drive and energy together with resources human and financial.
>
> At the end of it all, I am compelled to think that *Friends should use their faith to the utmost, but only advance their concerns after the acid test of ministry and the testing by the complete mechanism of the Quaker establishment* – I know of NO other faith or church which will allow a sinner like myself to go from the bottom to the top.[33]
>
> (Original italics and capitals)

This concern passed through the local meeting, through at least two meetings of the Monthly Meetings to the Peace and International Relations Committee and on to Meeting for Sufferings, the central executive body of the Society of Friends. The concern was tested by these – and maybe other – groups over six years, and by 1972 the Quaker Peace Studies Trust was set up, and an appeal launched to provide the additional finance. The Bradford School of Peace Studies was set up and is still going strong.

This is a typical, if dramatic, example of the working of a concern by Quakers. Many concerns cover a smaller canvas than this one, but are treated equally seriously. This principle of thoroughly testing a concern to see if it is really the will of God, and not just concern about something, is what has empowered Quaker work for the world over the last three hundred years, and enabled Friends to make an impact upon the world that is totally out of proportion to their small numbers.

A New Way of Working

Are your meetings for church affairs held in a spirit of worship and in dependence on ... God? [14]

I will never forget the first time I experienced a Quaker business meeting. I had been attending meeting for worship for some time, and was aware that, on the first Sunday of each month, after coffee, Friends would stay on for a business meeting. I assumed that it was just like another committee, fairly boring, and at that time I was not looking for any greater involvement with the meeting. However, I had found hints in my reading that the Quaker way of conducting such meetings was very different, and that I might ask for permission to attend. I did so, and they were delighted to encourage my interest.

Once coffee was over, and the washing-up completed, we went back into the meeting room, and immediately settled down to a deep silence. This went on for about ten minutes, when the clerk stood up and announced the start of the meeting. At first – apart from the silence at the beginning – it seemed like any other committee. Some minutes of the last meeting were read, and some routine items were also dealt with. However, I noticed that the minute for each agenda was read out and agreed at the time by the meeting as a whole, which was different to any experience I had at other meetings I had attended.

I was soon to see how different the Quaker way actually was. Up came an item of business – I forget exactly what it was – which seemed to merit some discussion. Though I cannot remember the details, the proceedings had an impact on me that I can recall to this day. It was one of those moments in my life that I can truthfully call a turning point. The effect of it was that I eventually decided to apply for membership.

Several Friends in turn put various points of view, and it seemed that a lively discussion was about to begin, when the clerk asked for a time of worship, and a deep silence descended once again. After a few minutes, a Friend who had not spoken previously stood up and summed up the main points of what had been said, but did not seem to say anything new. She sat down, and again there was a deep silence.

The clerk then said that she would try a minute. Hesitantly, she read, with several pauses for correction, what she felt the sense of the meeting had been. To my surprise, no-one challenged her, and even those who had been putting opposite points of view seemed to agree. I was later to learn that this was fairly usual. With a few small corrections to the wording, the minute was approved, and the meeting moved on.

To say that I was impressed would be an understatement. However I was not really any the wiser as to what had happened. I cannot say that I remember the rest of the meeting, or that it was equally impressive; it is just that I was in something of a daze. This one event seemed to me like an initiation. I have since attended many hundreds of Quaker business meetings, and have witnessed – I think I can fairly say – the best and the worst, but this first one was unique in my experience. I asked the librarian for a book on Quaker business meetings, and got a clue. Business meetings are actually 'Meetings for worship for business'.

The meeting for business cannot be understood in isolation; it is part of a spiritual discipline.
(John Punshon, QFP, 2.85)

John Punshon's statement sums up perfectly the essence of the Quaker business method. Business meetings (and the phrase 'business meetings' is shorthand for 'meetings for worship for business', but the full title should always be borne in mind) are yet another aspect of the whole Quaker approach to life. They are part of a philosophy that says that the individual is important; that we can be guided by the Spirit of God; and that this guidance possesses a wisdom that is often beyond our human ability to see.

Because no vote is taken, and because (ideally) every person is listened to and heard, however articulate or otherwise they may be, this is a unique way of working. Yet it is not unique to Quakers, but available to any group who are prepared to adopt similar principles.

In fact, Quakers are not alone in this approach to their everyday affairs. In his book, *Beyond Majority Rule; voteless decisions in the Religious Society of Friends*, Michael Sheeran tells how the Second Vatican Council of the Roman Catholic Church encouraged religious orders to practise renewal by getting in touch with their roots. The Jesuits, of which he is a member, discovered within their earliest documents a forgotten decision-making procedure called 'Communal Discernment'. Attempts to re-discover and practice this method led to Michael Sheeran's discovery of Quakers, and to his masterly study which is now published by Philadelphia Yearly Meeting in the USA.

Nor is it limited to 'official' Quaker groups. In India, there was a group in Calcutta which called itself Quaker, but was unknown to the mainstream of the Quaker world. Some Hindus, Moslem and Christians had found a copy of Robert Barclay's *Apology*, had discovered the way of silent worship, and met together regularly for over fifteen years. It was truly amazing that they managed to maintain a Quaker identity with only a few books to guide them.[34] They managed it because they regulated their affairs in the Quaker manner. There again, the Spirit of Truth is available to all who sincerely seek it, and It does not seem to mind what name It goes by.

The earliest clear record of a specifically Quaker style of business meeting is found in writing by Edward Burrough in 1662. He is talking about the London Business Meeting which was founded in 1655 to provide:

> ... convenient meeting places for the publishing of Truth,
> how the poor people that believed should be honestly taken
> care for, that no want should be amongst them; and that the
> sick and weak and impotent should be visited and provided
> for; and that such servants as were put away out of their ser-
> vices for receiving the Truth, should be looked after and
> placed in some honest employment.

Note that the business meeting considered both the spiritual
needs of the community, and also the needs of those who are
suffering. This combination has marked Quaker business
right up to the present time.

The way in which the meeting was conducted was singu-
lar, says Burrough. It was:

> Not in the way of the world, as a worldly assembly of
> men, by hot contests, by seeking to outspeak and over-
> reach one another in discourse, as it were in controversy
> between party and party of men, or two sides violently
> striving for dominion, in the way of carrying on some
> worldly interests for self-advantage, not deciding affairs
> by the greater vote, or the number of men, as the world,
> who have not the wisdom and power of God.

He goes on to say that the Quaker procedure meets in 'the
wisdom, love and fellowship of God', and in 'the holy Spirit
of truth' ... 'as only one party' ... 'assenting together as one
man in the spirit of truth and equity'.[35]

Allowing for the extravagances of seventeenth-century language, and the use of the word 'men' (when, today, there will
be both men and women at the meeting) this is as good a
description of the Quaker business method as you will find.

Because the meeting for business is also a meeting for worship, there is the need for all present to be in harmony. They will not be in harmony in their opinions, but in agreeing to seek God's will for the group, rather than force their opinions through by the strength of their arguments. We might think that Edward Burrough had parliament in mind. Imagine a parliament that sits in silence, that is not adversarial, that seeks unity in all decisions, where the opinions of each member have an equal weight and where members arrive with all this uppermost in their minds. We may well wonder what such a body might achieve.

Remember that we do not seek a majority decision or even consensus. As we wait patiently for divine guidance our experience is that the right way will open and we shall be led into unity. [14]

Any group of people who agree to do so can adopt the way of working described above. Maybe we will never see a parliament working in this way, but there are certainly moves in this direction in smaller committees throughout the Western world. There are groups without any religious overtones which practise something similar, and refer to it as 'consensus' or another term along the same lines. Working by consensus is valuable, but it is not the whole story. Sometimes Quaker business meetings operate in this way, though it is not the Quaker ideal. If it fully acknowledges the importance of each individual, and the group is prepared to work with great patience, then it is good. But there is a very subtle difference between consensus, unity and what Quakers call 'the sense of the meeting'. This is only realised when there is a sense of surrendering the outcome to a higher power. 'Thy will, not mine, be done' is the essence of our business method.

So, as with an ordinary meeting for worship, there is a significant element of experimentation in the Quaker business meeting. We are advised to come to any meeting for worship 'with heart and mind prepared'. The same thing applies to a business meeting. Heart and mind prepared means that we use our minds – recognised by Friends as a gift from God – to research thoroughly any material relating to what will be discussed. Preparing the heart means that we specifically refrain from making up our minds beforehand, and we come with some awareness of that of God within us.

It is possible to outline the major points for good business practice in the Quaker manner. The pattern is very clear, but requires some getting used to. A suggested 'checklist' might be:

- come to the meeting with an open mind and a sense of prayer
- practise deep listening, both to the contributions of others, and to your own inner voice.
- trust the working of the spirit within the meeting
- be prepared to speak only if you are sure you are prompted from within
- be patient and flexible
- trust that the decision taken by a meeting will be the right one

Of course, this is the ideal. But Quakers are human, and however much we are advised to come to a business meeting ' ... prepared to let your insights and personal wishes take their place alongside those of others or be set aside as the meeting seeks the right way forward' as well as with ' ... a generous and loving spirit'[15], this is not easy. We wouldn't be Quakers if we did not have an independent and questioning attitude to life. And this sort of outlook means that we have strong views on most things.

When it works, as obviously happened to those at the first business meeting I experienced, it is a thing of great wonder. It can be a life-changing experience. When it doesn't work, it is plain tedious. And much of the responsibility for this falls on the clerk.

When early Friends affirmed the priesthood of all believers it was seen as an abolition of the clergy; in fact it is the abolition of the laity. All members are part of the clergy and have the clergy's responsibility for the maintenance of the meeting as a community. (*QFP*, 11.01)

Though Friends have a major testimony to the 'priesthood of all believers', the organisation of a meeting does mean that certain people have to be appointed for a time to perform certain tasks. One of the major roles within a meeting is that of the clerk. The clerk is not a chairman nor a secretary, though he or she fulfils a part of both these roles. (As with all roles within the meeting, the clerk may be male or female.) The clerk is the person to whom all the information about events etc is sent, and who will often make the announcements at the end of the worship. But the clerk's most important role is in the business meeting.

The clerk has – to some extent – to control the meeting, though there may be elders present who will ensure that it is held in a spirit of worship. The clerk presents the items of business, ensures that there are adequate times of silence, and occasionally helps the meeting to move forward by summarising what has been said. When it becomes clear that a decision is near, the clerk will test the 'sense of the meeting' by drafting a minute. While the minute is being prepared, the other Friends present sit silently, upholding the process in prayer. Then the draft minute is read, and if it is accepted, that will be the recorded decision.

However, if there are those present who feel that it does not reflect the sense of the meeting, there will be further contributions, either correcting the minute or adding to it. Eventually, a minute may emerge which is acceptable. If it is, the meeting will approve it at the time, and move on to the next item. If not, then the clerk – and the meeting – may feel it right to minute that they are unable to come to a sense of unity, and the decision may be deferred to a later meeting to allow time for further reflection. Those who wish to follow the Quaker business method must be prepared to be patient, and part of the process of surrendering of our own will on any matter might be an acceptance that the time is not right for a decision.

On occasions I have come to a meeting with some prejudice, either for or against a particular course of action. As the meeting gathers, it has become clear that the majority share my point of view, but the eventual outcome has been the reverse, either because we are led to change our minds (and this is not always due to persuasive arguments) or because the sense of the meeting reveals that, even though many of those present *think* one thing, the clerk manages to discern that the *feeling* is towards the opposite.

This is an amazing process. I have clerked many business meetings, and one of the things that always astonishes me is the way things work out. They resolve themselves in ways that I could not have foreseen. Being a clerk at a good business meeting is like reading a really good whodunit. If the author knows their stuff, then there is no way we can discover the culprit until the end. Similarly, if we should be so rash as to turn to the end to see who committed the crime, we still have to finish reading the intervening chapters to see *how* it was done. And the how is often as interesting as the who.

My own experience is that when clerking a business meeting to which Friends have come with heart and mind prepared, there is a sharpening of the senses, and the intuitive faculty – our own still small voice – is also heightened. As I listen to Friends contributing, I may feel it right to insist on a time of silence between contributions. It is in this silence that the feeling often comes that the sense of the meeting – and the resulting minute – will be different from the prevailing view. But I do not know how until a Friend stands and says something that brings an even deeper silence to the meeting. Suddenly it is clear, and I feel moved to try a minute. The silence stays as I am writing it, and if I am lucky enough to have someone else at the table with me, they will help me. And then, suddenly, the minute is accepted and we move on.

Do you uphold those who are acting under concern, even
if their way is not yours? Can you lay aside your own
wishes and prejudices while seeking with others to find
God's will for them? (36)

For a group to work in this way, there needs to be a con-
siderable element of trust. It is no use complaining
afterwards if a meeting reaches a decision that we do not like.
We have to speak at the time, or trust the sense of the
meeting. Even more, if we are not present, we have to trust
those who are to come to the right decision. There may be
times when individuals are not happy with a decision and its
results. In the end, each one must be given the freedom to
follow their own conscience, though this does not mean that
they can 'veto' decisions reached by the meeting. The leadings of conscience can only tell *us* what *we* must do in any
particular circumstance. And for all their honest seeking,
Quakers *do* get it wrong sometimes.

The decision reached at a meeting is the one that is right
for that time and those people present. Time and consideration may change things. *Quaker Faith and Practice* tells us:

Friends should realise that a decision which is the only one
for a particular meeting may not be the one that is ultimately seen to be right. There have been many occasions
in our Society when a Friend, though maintaining his or
her personal convictions, has seen clearly that they were
not in harmony with the sense of the meeting and has with
loyal grace expressed deference to it. Out of just such a situation, after time for further reflection, an understanding

of the Friend's insight has been reached at a later date and has been ultimately accepted by the Society.[36]

Patience, understanding and flexibility are required for the Quaker method to work.

———◆◆◆———

> When words are strange or disturbing to you, try to sense where they come from and what has nourished the lives of others. Listen patiently and seek the truth which other people's opinions may contain for you. [17]

As with much of the Quaker way, the key is in listening. We have to learn to listen. We must listen to the details of what is being considered; listen to each other without judgement; and we must be quiet enough to listen to the Still Small Voice of the Spirit within us. If people are practised in meditation, or in Quaker worship, it is a great help. But the discipline of listening is something that can also be practised in everyday life. And it is a good skill to develop.

The technique of Creative Listening, discussed earlier is very helpful here. Rachel Pinney emphasised that the vital thing was that we learn to 'switch off the demanding self'. And it is this self which so often gets in our way. This ability is something that we can practise, and it is helpful if we take the time and trouble to do so.

There are two other developments of this technique which Quakers have evolved which are also very helpful here. They have evolved out of the Quaker business method, and involve the ability to listen deeply to each other. They have very specific applications, and have been widely used among Friends in the USA, They are now becoming increasingly used over here. They are called 'Worship Sharing' and 'Meetings for Clearness'. Quakers also hold special meetings for weddings, funerals and cremations and memorial meetings

Worship Sharing

In worship sharing, the idea of group creative listening is allied to the attitude of worship. It is a way that can be used for study, and to enable people who are shy and retiring to fully contribute to a discussion. The meeting gathers in an attitude of worship and, at a suitable time, the clerk will introduce the subject (if there is one). The meeting will then continue in silence, until someone feels moved to speak out of the silence. The others present listen in the same way as for a creative listening group, without judgement or the need to reply. Each person present will have the opportunity to speak from the silence in the same way, and no-one will speak twice. If anyone wishes not to speak, they are free to stay silent, but each person present is encouraged to feel that their views are important to the group. Eventually the meeting will close with silence. Worship sharing groups are often not seeking to come to any kind of a decision, and each person present will be able to take away with them those thoughts that they have personally found helpful.

The beauty of this practice is the space that it gives to each person present, empowering them to speak without any fear of being ridiculed or contradicted. In addition, the whole group feels the presence of the Spirit with it, and is able to respond according to their ability and need. It is an ideal way of discussing – if that is the right word – questions of belief, as the discipline frees all present to be themselves, and clarify in their own way what they really feel about a particular subject.

Meetings for Clearness

The other practice that has arisen out of the Quaker business method is that of Meetings for Clearness. Until recently, this practice was mostly found in the USA, but it is now becoming increasingly popular in the UK. It is ideal for considering, for example, whether the meeting should allow two people to marry under its care. In a meeting for clearness, the couple are encouraged to explore their relationship with one another, with the meeting and with God. They are also helped to look in depth at previous relationships and commitments, and the way in which they will live and work together in the future. It is rare for a meeting for clearness, on its own, to cause the meeting to refuse a request for a couple to marry under its care, although it might result in a suggestion that they wait or seek an alternative. In addition, the two people concerned might come to the conclusion that a Quaker wedding was not the right way for them, or reach some other decision about their future.

In a meeting for clearness, a group of people appointed for the purpose gather together to consider a particular proposal. They are usually people with skill in the Quaker method, but experience of life, prayer and meditation are also valuable. Clearness meetings are often held regarding practical matters relating to the meeting or an individual member. These may include marriages, relationships between people and with the meeting, membership matters, the testing of a concern, or the meeting's response to a request from another Quaker body for a particular course of action.

The meeting gathers in an attitude of worship, having first been reminded of the reason for the meeting. One member is usually appointed as facilitator, and it is explicitly stated that everything said in the meeting will be treated as confidential. People will only speak when they feel that they have something to say that sheds additional light upon the subject, or to seek clarification. Others will listen with full attention. All present are encouraged to be both honest and tender. It is important to keep to the subject, and not to be side-tracked. It takes time to reach clearness in such a way, and periods of silent gathered worship can be most helpful.

Groups of this kind are set up for one purpose only. When clearness has been reached, the group should be laid down (disbanded). Carrying forward the appropriate action is the responsibility of the meeting or the individual concerned.

Weddings and Funerals

———◆———

Quakers have special meetings for worship on two other occasions, for weddings and for funerals. Both are held in a similar manner, in the same quiet and simple form as a normal Quaker meeting for worship. They are often the first – and sometimes the only – contact that people have with Quakers, when they are invited to attend as guests. Most meetings allow for this, and if you are invited to either there will special leaflets available to explain the procedures.

Those who are married in the Quaker way are said to be 'Married under the care of the meeting'. This usually means that one or both parties will normally have something to do with the meeting. There are proper procedures for applying to have a wedding at a Quaker meeting.[37] The whole procedure is governed by legal requirements, and, from the moment application is made, the meeting as a whole takes responsibility for the marriage. Friends take this responsibility very seriously. Elders usually interview the couple, and may even organise a clearness meeting, particularly if they are not known to the meeting.

Because we have no priests or ministers, the couple make their vows to each other, to God and to the whole meeting. All present, members and guests, act as witnesses. Early in the course of the meeting, when they feel the time is right, the couple will stand and take each other by the hand, and each will make a similar promise:

Friends, I take this my friend, XXX, to be my wife/hus-
band, promising, with God's help (or with Divine
assistance) to be unto her/him a loving and faithful hus-
band/wife as long as we both shall live. [38]

There is usually a special Quaker wedding certificate, which
everyone present will be invited to sign, and which many
couples frame and put on the wall of their home.

The meeting continues for the allotted time with a further
time of silent worship, in which there will probably be some
ministry relevant to the occasion. It is a solemn yet joyous
occasion, dignified yet simple, and an experience that
enriches the lives of all present, and brings a real blessing on
the couple and their marriage.

Funerals, cremations and memorial meetings are held in a
similar way. They are also held in silent worship, and can be
in the meeting house, at the crematorium, or by the grave-
side. All present gather in silence, and the emphasis is on a
remembrance of the departed, and in praying for those who
are bereaved. The silence may be broken by ministry, often
referring to the life of the deceased. Anyone present may
speak if they are moved to do so.

Quakers have a special way of talking about a person's life
which relates to the way we are inspired by the everyday life
of departed Friends. We say we 'Give thanks for the grace of
God in the life of ... ' a person. We do not separate their spiritual and material lives, for we know that all is due to the
grace of God, and that the quality of that life is measured by
the extent to which that grace is radiated to touch the lives of
others.

Quakers do not normally have special meetings for other events or rites of passage in a life. However, some meetings or groups of Friends will hold a special meeting to celebrate events such as the birth of a child or the acceptance of someone into membership. There have also been occasions where a special meeting was held to help come to terms with a divorce, or for the loss of a foetus in the early stages of pregnancy. These special meetings are sometimes in the nature of celebration, and sometimes as a meeting for healing, depending on the need. As there is no set ceremony, the form of the meeting can be adapted to meet specific needs, and sometimes meaningful events are introduced, such as lighting candles, special readings, or the playing of music. So long as the simple silence of the regular meeting is the foundation on which they are built, these additions do not interfere with the basis of Quaker worship, which is openness to the deep (and healing) silence of the spirit.

As with all such meetings, it is the Spirit that brings a benediction to the occasion. It is important to remember that whatever the intention, these are still meetings for worship. Awareness of the Divine is what allows the occasion to be blessed, so we must be certain that this is our first priority. Marking the important events of life in such a simple yet profound way has great potential. But it could be abused. This is why, particularly for weddings, there are regulations that may seem rather severe. Quakers emphasise discipline and dignity at such times to prevent an 'anything goes' situation. The rules are there to ensure that the whole of the worshipping community can give its wholehearted support.

———◦•◦———

Do you consider difficult questions with an informed
mind as well as a generous and loving spirit? Are you prepared to let your insights and personal wishes take their
place alongside those of others or be set aside as the meeting seeks the right way forward? (15)

The Quaker business method has an almost infinite
potential. Much of it has not even been realised by
Friends themselves, and it may be up to others to explore the
method further, extend its boundaries, and adapt it to their
own needs. To be able to reach decisions without voting, and
where all concerned are seeking to co-operate for the greater
good, is something that should make anyone hold their
breath, just in case it might work. To realise that it often
does, and that this way of working can apply to both small
and big matters, is little short of amazing. Yet the basic principle must always be remembered – that we are seeking the
will and understanding of a higher power than ourselves, and
that we are prepared to surrender our own thoughts, feeling
and prejudices in order that the right result may come about.

This is not easy. It has not been easy for Friends through
the years, and it will not be easy for anyone who tries to
follow it in the future. However, Quakers know that there is
a Guiding Light that will show us the way forward, if we are
prepared to let It. If we are willing to first learn to be aware
of our thoughts and prejudices and to surrender them, and
then to practice the principles of inner and outer listening,
this new way of working has great promise for the future,
and who knows what the future may hold: only God.

THE ADVENTUROUS LIFE

True faith is not assurance, but the readiness to go forward
experimentally, without assurance. It is a sensitivity to things
not yet known. Quakerism should not claim to be a religion
of certainty, but a religion of uncertainty; it is this which
gives us our special affinity to the world of science. For what
we apprehend of truth is limited and partial, and experience
may set it all in a new light; if we too easily satisfy our urge
for security by claiming that we have found certainty, we
shall no longer be sensitive to new experiences of truth. For
who seeks that which he believes he has found? Who ex-
plores a territory which he claims already to know?
(Charles Carter, 1971, *QFP*, 26.39)

I can look back now over the years of my spiritual journey
through life, and feel that I have been very fortunate. It
did not always seem so at the time. My early life in the
Roman Catholic Church felt very difficult, as I could not get
answers to those questions that deeply troubled me. And my
biggest problem was probably that of faith. And this is a
problem that many have today.

It is only now, after years of reading. studying and meditating that I am beginning to get an inkling of what faith really is. For many years I was convinced that I did not have it. I was not unhappy with this, until people told me I must have it. I was taught, as many people were, that faith was synonymous with belief. Further, in religious matters, it meant belief in the impossible, and suspension of the rational mind. When I was young, I went to the priest – in fact, a number of priests – and asked about faith. They mentioned certain essential points of doctrine that I must believe in to be saved. But I could not accept that a God of Love needed the sacrifice of His Son for my sins. It did not – and still does not – make sense to me.

I was told quite firmly that if I did not have faith I was doomed; destined after death to spend eternity in hell – and the picture painted of hell was not a pretty one to a young mind. For some reason, I was not afraid. Rather, I was even more puzzled. I knew that St John had told us that 'God is Love', and this I knew to be true (how I cannot tell you). Anything that did not resonate with what I knew as love could not be true. I *could* not believe it. I *did* not believe it. And I did not want anything to do with religion if it demanded that I have that kind of faith.

The Christian churches are not alone in encouraging this attitude. I found this when I discovered Buddhism. Buddhism is a deeply compassionate religion, but some of its scriptures have visions of hell that are at least as horrific as the Christian ones. But there is a difference. Buddhist hells are not for ever. The teaching of rebirth ensures there is always another chance.

Though I recently heard a learned professor of Buddhism state that the rational mind is the source of our evil passions, Buddhism is predominantly a rational religion. My first introduction came after I had left the Roman church, when I heard a monk speaking about the *Kalama Sutta*, where the Buddha told the Kalama people not to believe anything because it was written in a holy book, a priest said it, or even because he, the Buddha, taught it. He told them only to accept those things that made life more peaceful and harmonious, that pointed the way out of suffering and brought about the welfare of all beings.

This was just what I needed to hear, and it helped me to return to the spiritual path at a time when I thought I was in danger of rejecting all forms of religion. (Although I now think that this would not have happened, as I recognise that I am, by nature, a religious animal.) Then, as I have said earlier, I found the Quakers. I discovered that there was such a thing as a Christian group teaching that we should value personal spiritual experience, a group that did not demand acceptance of any creeds; in fact, one that did not demand faith. I later learned that there are those (including the foremost Catholic theologian, Thomas Aquinas) who consider that faith is a gift from God. As with all God's gifts, you have it wholly, in part, or you don't have it at all. To discover Quakerism which values equally faith, trust, personal experience and reason was a great liberating experience for me.

I have been very fortunate to be able to travel my spiritual journey with Friends, and I am grateful to many of them. I have found some wonderful companions on the journey. Some are from the seventeenth and eighteenth centuries, and these I can only know from writings, but many of their thoughts are relevant and helpful for me today. Other spiritual friends are here in the body, and I have been fortunate to get to know some of them as F/friends. Their living examples confirm all that I have read, even though I do not know one tenth of the whole of their stories.

I hope that so far I have managed to convey a picture of Quaker Life and thought today, and also of the essence behind it. The lives and the thoughts have changed over three hundred years, but the essence has not. Contemporary Quakers are inspired by the writings of early Friends, but do not make the mistake of thinking that everything written by, for example, George Fox, is relevant for today. We live in a different world; we know a great deal more about it and its make-up, and we have possibilities of communication and travel that could not have been imagined even a hundred years ago, to say nothing of three.

Quakers have discovered that there is within each person something of the Divine. This is not just a small spark; it is our life, our being, and awareness of it is capable of transforming our lives in ways that we could not ever have thought possible. This is not just an empty theory. Neither is it about placating some God who is separate from us. Rather, it reveals that the Divine is so much a part of us that St Paul could say: 'I live, but not I; Christ liveth in me.'[39] Many lives have been changed for the better through the discovery and application of this truth.

In order to discover this for ourselves, we do not have to believe that it is so. If we are prepared to approach the subject with an open mind that is prepared to admit that it has not had any experience of God, but is willing to explore and find out, then we can commence our search. We need to honestly say, 'I don't know', with no 'buts'. This leads to a quiet mind, and one of the best ways to carry out the spiritual search is through silence. If we are able to listen, we will find that the silence is by no means empty.

For a Quaker, religion is not an external activity concerning a special 'holy' part of the self. It is an openness to the here and now with the whole of the self ... In short, to put it in traditional language, there is no part of ourselves and of our relationships where God is not present.
(Harvey Gillman, *QFP*, 20.20)

Life, the spiritual and physical journey of each of us, is unique. It is also something that we share with the rest of humanity. Whatever the pattern of our lives, there is a space within us where inspiration and intuition function if we will let them. Our minds and our reason are important, but so is this inner space, for it is here that the Light shines in the darkness.

It will be clear by now that for me the deepest essence of Quakerism lies in the ability to listen deeply. This is not unique to Quakerism, but Quakers have found unique ways of expressing it. What they have done is to emphasise the balance between listening to the Light Within, and to Life around us – which includes people. And often we need to do both at the same time. In doing so we find that the words of St John's Gospel are literally true; that in this world the Light and the Life are one.

The Light does not need to speak in words, for when it is there, we know it, though at times it is so subtle that we have to wait longer to be sure. Although we sometimes hear it as a still small voice, it often comes as a sense of the release of our burdens, or a deep feeling that we are not alone. Birthright Friends, those who were born into Quaker families, tended in the past to absorb this ability to listen inwardly from their earliest years, almost without trying. But even within Quaker families, most people today need to find ways in which they can slow down and be centred enough to give their attention to that of the Divine at the heart of their being.

If you have been inspired by the picture of Quaker Life given so far, how do you start to live it? There are a number of things that you can do, starting with the most simple and direct. You can:

- try to practise a simple listening (contemplative) meditation (*see* below)
- practise listening to other people in the way outlined in the section on Creative Listening (*see* page 109)
- attend a local Quaker meeting for worship
- look at the section on Testimonies (page 150), and see if any of them immediately appeal to you
- write for more information (*see* Useful Addresses)
- read the *Advices and Queries* (*see* Appendix 1)

I would like to highlight one or two of these possibilities.

Contemplative Meditation

What is my religion? My friends, my teachers, my God.
And who is my God? He speaks within me; if I mishear,
my friends correct me; if I misdo, I look to Jesus Christ.
How then am I taught? I hear in the silence, I ponder in
solitude, and I try in the noisy crowd to practise it.
(Frederick Parker-Rhodes, 1977, *QFP*, 26.41)

I have said repeatedly that for me the key is listening, so let us look at one way in which this can be developed. This is through contemplative meditation. I have taught groups and workshops in meditation to many different people. Most of them start with misconceptions. They think – among other things – that meditation is Eastern and exotic; that it involves making the mind a blank; that they need to be able to sit on the floor; that it is non-Christian, or that it is only for the few. Some complain that when they try to meditate, they cannot concentrate, that they fall asleep or that they 'feel funny'.

None of these relate to the simple technique of contemplative meditation. This meditation is especially suited for the Western mind, firmly rooted in the Judeo-Christian tradition (though also found in others), and can be performed anywhere and in any posture that is comfortable. (Even in Buddhism, the Buddha said that there were four postures for meditation: sitting, standing, walking and lying down. But this is usually ignored.)

Furthermore, contemplative meditation recognises that it is almost impossible for us to make the mind a blank. The phenomenon of the 'monkey mind' already referred to in the section on worship equally applies to meditation. To make the mind blank is not even an ideal. If you could do it, you would be left with the thought of a blank mind, which is just as much a thought as anything else. Contemplative meditation encourages the mind to do its work. It recognises that reason is also a Divine gift, and so *uses* the thought processes to take us to a place of peace. It recognises that the quiet mind is a gift of God, a fruit of grace, which is given to us 'not as the world giveth', and it provides a means whereby we can accept the gift gratefully.

I would like to suggest a way that you can start, but can adapt to your own needs as they become clear. Choose a favourite passage from scripture (any scripture), or an inspirational piece of poetry or prose. As an example, and because we have already mentioned it, I will use the phrase 'God is Love'. My mind might work along these lines:

God is Love …
How do I know this?
Is it just because it is in the Bible?
Or is there another way I can know it?
Think for a moment about Love …
Those times when I have experienced Love in my life, how did I feel?
They were the times when I felt safe, cared for, at peace with the world.
Is there any more sublime feeling than being totally, unconditionally loved?
If God is Good, All-Good, then surely He or She must

be Loving. It would not make sense for such a God to make conditions, and so God's Love must be unconditional.

In fact, Love and God are One ...

Looking at it this way makes sense of the parables of Jesus of the Lost Sheep or the Prodigal Son ...

Thinking about this helps me to feel loved!

And how about the times when I feel love for somebody?

Mostly, it is because they love me.

That's all right, makes me feel good, but ...

Sometimes, just sometimes, this happens in spite of, and not because of, what they have done. Logically I should not feel love at such times, but I recognise that it is there in spite of what I may think or feel.

Love is within me, and will flow out if I do not block it.

This love within me is God ...

The above is only a suggestion as to how your mind might work. It is not a formula, though you can read it through slowly to get a feel. Meditation is your experience, and if it is to be creative, then what happens to your thoughts as you allow them to flow within you is what is important. If I were to try the same meditation it would almost certainly be different, as yours will be each time you try it.

This is only the preliminary stage. The next is the most important. You have used your mind to consider every aspect of the chosen subject. You have channelled it into thoughts of the Divine, and you have allowed inspiration to rise with ideas that might have escaped your normal reasoning. Slowly, very slowly, in its own time, the mind runs out of thoughts. A stillness will settle in which there is a sense of deep listening. It is like a muddy pool. The only way to clear it is to leave it alone. You cannot *do* anything to make it clear, but if you leave it, the mud will settle. I could compare it to walking on the Downs near the sea and, when the wind turns, just catching the strains of a band playing somewhere in the distance. If we rest in that listening stillness, we may hear an inner voice, or catch a sense of deep peace or release of tensions.

Some people would call this prayer, and indeed it is that too. It is the prayer of the disciples who asked, 'Lord, teach us to pray.' It is a prayer of affirmation, of realising that the way we see God is the way that we see ourselves, as 'That of God' is an integral part of us, or rather, we are an integral part of God. It is the movement from prayer with words to the prayer of silence.

If you are tired, and need sleep, then sleep may come. We should not resist it but accept it gratefully. In fact, not resisting it often tends to disperse the tendency to fall asleep while meditating. Most systems of meditation teach that sleep is to be avoided at all costs, but God is not any less God, not any less present, because we go to sleep. If that were so, then a third of our lives would be spent without God. And if, as Quakers say, God is within us as well as 'out there', then our dream world is also a manifestation of the Divine. Besides, our meditation is intended to bring us what we need to make our lives whole, so if you need sleep, sleep well.

Above all, remember that this approach to meditation is perfectly natural. It is our nature to want to contemplate the mysteries of life. This approach uses our faculties, and takes us deeper than the senses can. We may not find the big answers, but we can find answers for ourselves and for a particular time. These may change as our understanding deepens, but we must accept that we can never know everything that is to be known, even about a simple flower. This type of meditation can also be performed through looking deeply into something, like a flower or a stone, and seeking to discover its meaning for us.

Whatever way we approach it, contemplative meditation is a good basis for our daily lives. It is also helpful in our approach to the other basic fount of inspiration within Quakerism, the Meeting for Worship.

Meeting for Worship.

To me, worship is recognising and communing with the
divine, whether it is within myself, in others, or in the
world. The pre-condition of worship is my belief in
worth-ship, my own and that of other people. (A member
of the Quaker Women's Group, *QFP*, 2.08)

As I said right at the beginning, this book has not been written to persuade anybody to become a Quaker. Its purpose is much more than that. If I can share some of the depth of inspiration that I have found through Quakers past and present, and if it is helpful, then that is enough. However, I still feel that to really understand what Quakers are about, you need to attend a meeting for worship that is really gathered. And as Quaker worship is experimental, this may mean attending more than one meeting.

I hope that if you have read thus far you will have some idea what to expect. I will try to give you a little more. But no-one can tell you what will happen. People have come to worship in this way because they have found something which is priceless; something that has become a vital part of their lives. In a simple silent gathering they have experienced the presence of God in a unique way, uncluttered with rituals, creeds, set prayers and priests or ministers. Some Quakers confess to missing music and song in their worship, yet they would not wish to change the pattern of meeting, even though they may need to go elsewhere at times.

If you do go to a meeting you may find it easy to relax into the silence from the beginning, or you may feel a little disturbed by the strangeness of what is happening (or perhaps what is not happening). Do not worry about it, but try to turn your thoughts to God, or towards whatever it is that you think of as highest and best in life. If you do not believe in God, or if you are unsure, do not worry. You are not expected to believe anything until you have had the experience. There are no creeds to sign up to. Come to the meeting just as you are, bringing the whole of your joys, sorrows, searches and discoveries into the stillness.

It may seem strange to say that you do not have to believe in God when you have come to a meeting the purpose of which is worship. But a Quaker Meeting for Worship's first aim is to find God. Even those who believe in or have experienced God in their lives, come to the meeting to find God. If

God is Infinite and Eternal, as we are told, we cannot encompass that with our human minds. Yet our gateway to this Infinity is in the Here, and to Eternity in the Now, and that is why we must find God each day, and each time we worship. Quakers do not believe we can worship that which we do not know, or which is just contained in words from the past.

Listen into the silence. You will hear sounds, possibly of birds or traffic outside, or of somebody fidgeting in another part of the room. In some old meeting houses there is the ticking of a clock, or the creaking of ancient benches. Do not judge these and other sounds as either good or bad, but accept them for what they are; just sounds of various kinds. Trying to shut them out is pointless, as resisting them in this way only increases their power to disrupt your thoughts. As you come to accept them, just as you would wish to be accepted, then they will cease to trouble you, and you will be able to hear the silence. After a while, it is as if you can hear through the silence, but after that the experience is yours, and neither I nor anyone else can tell you how it will be. You have to find God in your own way.

A Quaker meeting for worship is in some ways like many other spiritual groups, and in other ways it is unique. Meetings vary greatly. No two are the same, and no-one can guarantee that you will get what you need from it. I do know that it is an experience that I do not hesitate to recommend to anyone who is a spiritual seeker, and one which many have found helpful, either by providing a new spiritual home, or by being the means of pointing the way towards one.

Testimonies

—◆—

Testimonies are not imposed on members of the Society of
Friends, but they are re-affirmed corporately and re-ex-
pressed sufficiently often to be both a challenge and a way
of living for most Friends. They do not make it any easier
to live a life of faithfulness to God's leadings, for they give
rise to many dilemmas and compromises as we live in a
society which is often based on other presuppositions.
(Chris Lawson, 1987, QFP, 20.17)

We have seen how the Quaker life is composed of the
inner listening, both in meeting for worship and in
private, and of guided action in the world. The testimonies
are often seen as being just concerned with the latter, but this
is not so. Look at some of the testimonies, and say whether
you feel they would be a good guide for your life:

- peace and non-violence
- truth and integrity
- simplicity in living
- honesty in our dealings with others
- avoiding gambling and speculation
- avoiding excesses
- equality
- sharing of our resources
- care for the planet

I expect that you will agree that most of these are good ideals,
and maybe you would like to make some of them your own.

There is nothing wrong in this; indeed, adopting any of these principles as a guide to life must be a good thing. Of course there is another dimension. How will you live up to them? What will be your guidelines for deciding which ones are right for you, and how you will carry them forward and stay with them? This is where the spiritual dimension comes in.

Let us look at examples and consider what is involved. In the testimony to peace and non-violence, what would be your attitude if your country was at war, and you were liable to call-up into the armed forces? You have a number of choices. You can refuse to have anything to do with it, in which case you will probably be arrested and put into gaol. You can seek to become a registered conscientious objector (if the law allows for such a status), and you will probably be given work on the land, in a factory or a hospital. If the latter, do you agree to work in a military hospital or not? You may be willing to join the forces, provided you can work in a medical corps or something similar. If you do this, are you willing to carry arms if you are sent to the front line? Or you may feel that the evil you are fighting against is so bad that you have no alternative but to fight, even though you believe in peace. There are a great number of such questions to be answered, and no-one can answer then for you.

In the two world wars, Quakers had these and many other decisions to make. Often, their lives were literally laid on the line for their principles. In today's world, British Quakers at least are not called upon to make such extreme decisions, but we may have to make decisions that are socially difficult, cause us financial loss, or affect our career or life-style. For example, might a testimony lead us to move out of a secure and financially rewarding job in the arms trade, or some other business that exploits people or the planet? Might it make us withdraw investments from firms that support the making of armaments? Could it be that for us non-violence includes becoming a vegetarian or even a vegan?

These and similar decisions are not made lightly. They are arrived at only after much thought and prayer. They may mean that we have to change our interests, our friends or our church. Imagine being part of a regular dining club who go out for regular steak meals. How do you break the news that you feel led to become a vegetarian, and still retain the friend-ship of the group? Such a thing is not impossible. For five years I was London Secretary of the Vegetarian Society, and I had to make a similar decision. Did I continue to eat out with my old friends, regardless of the fact that they were all meat-eaters, or did I lose my friends? In the end, I decided to try to keep my friends, and yet eat vegetarian. As it turned out, this was the right decision. I was careful to ask quietly for vege-tarian food, and not to preach in any way. My actions were seen as non-threatening, and friends often insisted that we eat in a wholefood establishment, or joined me in a vegetarian banquet at our local Indian restaurant.

An additional factor in making life-changing decisions is the support of a community. Among Quakers, the support of the meeting is very significant. Inspirations – even personal ones with no wider implications – can be tested with a group that we have learned to trust. This does not have to be the whole meeting, or even a part of it. Any group of friends who will agree to meet in silence to consider a problem can be of tremendous help when we are faced with the possibility of life-changing decisions. If you should decide to join the Quakers, you would only be encouraged to do so after you have attended meetings for some time. Even then, this decision is tested as rigorously as any, for it is vital that the applicant knows what they are letting themselves in for. There can also be family problems when only one member of a household decides to join.

The advice is; take it slowly. As with ministering at meeting, wait until you are sure that you are being pushed towards a particular testimony, and above all, do not leap in and feel you have a mission to preach to a world that doesn't want to listen, and doesn't really care. Some of the testimonies, such as that to simplicity or truth, can be entered into gradually. We need only to watch our behaviour and our reactions carefully, so that we can change a little at a time. Remember that a testimony to truth means that *each* time we speak we should be aware of what we are saying, and of its effect on ourselves and others. A testimony to simplicity can be embraced by consciously simplifying one aspect of our lives at a time, taking space to check our inner guidance for a feeling of rightness.

The world often does not take kindly to the putting of our lives into what Quakers call 'Right ordering'. If we are sure that what we wish to do is right, and we allow others to help us in the testing of it, then we can stand against the world if it becomes necessary. But we do not do this lightly. In recent years, some Friends have felt it right to refuse to pay that portion of their taxes that is spent on armaments. This has not become a testimony for the whole of the Society of Friends, because there are other Quakers who – though they

feel just as strongly about the question of war and armaments – are certain that this is not the right way forward.
Divisions can occur, but such is the unity of the shared
worship, that it is usually acceptable for each one to follow
their conscience in similar matters.

Simplicity

───────•◆•───────

Every stage of our lives offers fresh opportunities.
Responding to divine guidance, try to discern the right
time to undertake or relinquish responsibilities without
undue pride or guilt. Attend to what love requires of you,
which may not be great busyness [28]

Another of the Quaker testimonies that we can do
something about is that to simplicity. In today's world,
there are few people who can say that their lives are really
simple. Most of us need to simplify our lives. When we first
hear about the ideal of simplicity, it easily finds a place in our
hearts. Secretly, most of us yearn for a less involved lifestyle.
If we can identify the areas which complicate and clutter our
existence, this can be the first step to discovering whether we
really need to keep them.

The vision of the simple life is so attractive that there is a
danger of over-reaction. This is where the Quaker approach is
helpful. We can feel so overwhelmed by this modern lifestyle
and all the things that seem absolutely vital, that either we
cannot think where to start, or there is a temptation to be

quick and ruthless so that we do not hang on to things 'just in case'. It is important not to succumb to either extreme.

As we have seen in other examples, we should not do anything just because we think it is a good idea. Life is so complex, that what is a good idea for some, is a disaster for others. We can be fairly sure that there are certain areas of our lives that we can let go, but we need to be sure of what it is right for us to surrender. This is not only for ourselves; there are other people to consider. It may prove easy for us to think of things that we would like to get rid of in our lives; that we do not need, and which we managed perfectly well without before we had them. However, some of these may actually make our lives easier in a positive way, giving us the time and ability to fulfil our own potential, and maybe benefit the world. It is a question of balance.

The Quaker approach is to take changes slowly, making sure that we are in agreement with the Spirit within. This inner harmony will lead us to the type of true simplicity that is right for us, and also for all those whose lives touch ours, known and unknown. To take one example, we might feel that we spend too much time watching television, or even that we no longer need to own one. Should we get rid of it altogether, thereby affecting the lives of other members of the family who may not have the same needs as us, or develop the self-discipline to view selectively, and to spend time doing something else while others are watching? Our own minds are not capable of knowing all the detailed ramifications of any changes we might decide to make, or what might happen in the future. The Quaker way is to allow the Spirit to decide, and then all will be well.

Of course people have made mistakes in thinking they are doing God's will, and ruining their own lives and those of others around them. This is why it is vital to proceed slowly, to learn to follow your intuitions in small things which only affect you until you are able to trust the Inner Voice absolutely.

Practically, how can we do this? I suggest starting by writing lists. To externalise our thoughts on such matters is to clarify them. Write two lists; one, of the things that you think you can live without, and the other of those you feel are essential in your life. There may be some things, such as books, which come into both categories. You can include them in both, for when you come to look at them again, it will be obvious what to do with them.

Now start with the first list, the things you feel you can let go. This list can include physical things, personal attitudes and practices. Try and ensure the list has a mixture of all three. Pick out one item from the list. Consider carefully and contemplatively what place it has in your life. Take time to listen in stillness to see if there are any intuitive thoughts that you had not been consciously aware of. If it still feels clear that you can live without it, then resolve to do so for a week. (If that does not seem sufficient, try a fortnight or a month). At the end of that time, review the situation, and decide whether you will let go permanently.

It may seem that this way of doing things is too slow, and that it will take forever to simplify your life. But consider, even if you take a month to decide, at the end of a year you have shed twelve unnecessary parts of your life, which you had thought essential before.

As for the other list, keep this for later consideration. When your life has become less complicated, then take this other list and treat it in a similar way, considering whether everything on it should actually be there. Do not worry if you do not feel moved to make any changes at first. Keep it by you, and read it through slowly and carefully, from time to time pausing for periods of silent listening. Suddenly, one day, one or more items on this second list will seem unimportant, and you can then try living without them. Simplicity has become a part of your life!

An Adventurous Life

Perhaps the most neglected of the Advices is that we should live adventurously. If there is one that I would pray the Spirit to put into our Christmas stockings, it is warmth, openness, passion, a bit of emotion that doesn't mind making a fool of itself occasionally. (Gerald Priestland, 1977, QFP, 21.25)

Viewed from the outside, Quakers give the impression of being stolid, serious and slightly dull. Actually, nothing could be further from the truth. The Friends, friends in every sense, with whom I have travelled my spiritual journey are creative, imaginative, and possessed of a great sense of humour. If Friends were given to creating a public relations image for themselves – which, thank heaven, they are not – then it would seem that there is a lot of work to do.

Why is it that Quakers project this image? I think there are three reasons. Firstly, their values are different from much of the world around them. In fact, there are probably thousands of people who feel the same way, but have not necessarily articulated it in the way that Friends have done over nearly three hundred and fifty years. One of the great gifts of silence is that once you are comfortable with it, it teaches you to value the real things of life. Quakers have added to this the insight that, in the silence, we can find ways to act that will have real and positive effects on the world's exploitation and suffering.

The second point is an extension of the first. Quakers have learned that there is nothing so valuable as the experience of the presence and action of God in every aspect of our lives. In fact, our lives are incomplete without it, and in its absence, they are incapable of real fulfilment. However, we do not make the mistake of thinking that only Quakers, or even Christians, have the only access to this Divine inspiration and energy. Nor do we deny that others have found it through their own ways of worship. We acknowledge that there are many people of all faiths and none who have also discovered this truth in their own way, and use their own language to express it. Even people who would never wish to use the word 'God' may still recognise something beyond their conscious selves which inspires and motivates them.

Friends value the depth of their inner experience, and the power that it has over their lives. If they live life with half an ear to the Inner Voice, or half an eye to the Light Within, then they may seem to be not of this world. In fact, the ideal is to be ' ... in the world but not of it'. This does not mean that we fail to appreciate the good things of life, but that we appreciate that the vital joy of these gifts is enhanced by recognition that they are the Grace of God manifest. As Jesus said, 'It is your Father's good pleasure to give you the kingdom.'[40] We have the kingdom, not to abuse or exploit, but to enjoy.

The third problem that Quakers have is that in many people's minds they are associated with the past. It is true that most Friends have a great sense of history, and also that much of our inspiration comes from the insights of the practical mysticism of early Friends. It is also true that some of our language is taken from the seventeenth and eighteenth centuries. However, Quakers today are as much concerned with the present and the future as the past. The nature of our meeting for worship is based on the acceptance that our experience will be a 'Now' one. And much of the Quaker work in the world is concerned with the future. As a relatively small group we are not able to tackle the world's grand disasters – though we do try to help – but are more concerned with building foundations to ensure that similar ones do not occur in the future.

It is not clear what Friends can do to change these misconceptions. The Quaker way is a living stream which is available to anyone who wishes to drink from it. We need to be careful that this stream remains pure, and that we do not pollute it with too many worldly ideals and values. We also need to offer this water freely to any who are thirsty for spiritual nourishment, and not worry whether they end up by calling themselves 'Quakers'.

It might seem to be a risk to share our discoveries without thought of what may return to us, but this is just what we must do. Quakers do not always live up to their own advice to 'Live adventurously'. We are as guilty as anyone of trying to find certainty, but such a thing does not exist in today's world. The apparent certainties of the past no longer satisfy today's seekers. We all know so much about the world, its make-up, its thought and its practices that we cannot be satisfied with the explanations of yesterday. The only certainty is the living power of the Spirit, which constantly changes to meet our needs with unconditional love. Since the seventeenth century, Quakers have been sharing their discovery that it can still be experienced directly by anyone who is prepared to wait with an open heart and mind, willing to follow whatever is received. The message is still the same today.

APPENDIX

The Advices
and
Queries

The Advices and Queries *is a potted guidebook to the Quaker Life. It was originally a set of questions which were read out at meetings to allow Friends to be sure that they were acting in a way that was distinctively Quaker, and that they were following the Quaker testimonies. Today, it is still used in this way, but is also read regularly by individual Friends as a reminder of those things that are distinctively Quaker.*

Over the years, the contents of Advices and Queries *has been altered and revised approximately every twenty to twenty-five years to meet the needs of the time, while retaining its specific Quaker content. This alteration has usually been done by a specially appointed committee, but any Friend was allowed to submit suggestions. The amended version was then considered by the Yearly Meeting, amended where necessary, and then approved for use.*

The present version is a part of Quaker Faith and Practice, *which is* The Book of Christian discipline of the Yearly Meeting of the Religious Society of Friends (Quakers) in Britain. *The book, including the* Advices, *was approved at Yearly Meeting in 1994, and is published as part of QFP and also as a separate booklet. It is reproduced here by permission of the Yearly Meeting.*

Appendix

INTRODUCTION

As Friends we commit ourselves to a way of worship which allows God to teach and transform us. We have found corporately that the Spirit, if rightly followed, will lead us into truth, unity and love: all our testimonies grow from this leading.

Although the corporate use of *Advices and Queries* is governed by more flexible regulations ... than in the past, they should continue to be a challenge and inspiration to Friends in their personal lives and in their life as a religious community which knows the guidance of the universal spirit of Christ, witnessed to in the life and teachings of Jesus of Nazareth.

Advices and Queries is not a call to increased activity by each individual Friend but a reminder of the insights of the Society. Within the community there is a diversity of gifts. We are all therefore asked to consider how far the *Advices and Queries* affect us personally and where our own service lies. There will also be diversity of experience, of belief and of language. Friends maintain that expressions of faith must be related to personal experience. Some find traditional Christian language full of meaning; some do not. Our understanding of our own religious tradition may sometimes be enhanced by insights of other faiths. The deeper realities of our faith are beyond precise verbal formulation and our way of worship based on silent waiting testifies to this.

Our diversity invites us both to speak what we know to be true in our lives and to learn from others. Friends are encouraged to listen to each other in humility and understanding, trusting in the Spirit that goes beyond our human effort and comprehension. So it is for the comfort and discomfort of Friends that these *Advices and Queries* are offered, with the hope that we may all be more faithful and find deeper joy in God's service.

> *Dearly beloved Friends, these things we do not lay upon you as a rule or form to walk by, but that all, with the measure of light which is pure and holy, may be guided; and so in the light walking and abiding, these may be fulfilled in the Spirit, not from the letter, for the letter killeth, but the Spirit giveth life.* (Postscript to an epistle to 'the brethren in the north' issued by a meeting of elders at Balby, 1656.)

Advices and Queries

1. Take heed, dear Friends, to the promptings of love and truth in your hearts. Trust them as the leadings of God whose Light shows us our darkness and brings us to new life.

2. Bring the whole of your life under the ordering of the spirit of Christ. Are you open to the healing power of God's love? Cherish that of God within you, so that this love may grow in you and guide you. Let your worship and your daily life enrich each other. Treasure your experience of God, however it comes to you. Remember that Christianity is not a notion but a way.

3. Do you try to set aside times of quiet for openness to the Holy Spirit? All of us need to find a way into silence which allows us to deepen our awareness of the Divine and to find the inward source of our strength. Seek to know an inward stillness, even amid the activities of daily life. Do you encourage in yourself and in others a habit of dependence on God's

guidance for each day? Hold yourself and others in the Light, knowing that all are cherished by God.

4.   The Religious Society of Friends is rooted in Christianity and has always found inspiration in the life and teachings of Jesus. How do you interpret your faith in the light of this heritage? How does Jesus speak to you today? Are you following Jesus' example of love in action? Are you learning from his life the reality and cost of obedience to God? How does his relationship with God challenge and inspire you?

5.   Take time to learn about other people's experiences of the Light. Remember the importance of the Bible, the writings of Friends and all writings which reveal the ways of God. As you learn from others, can you in turn give freely from what you have gained? While respecting the experiences and opinion of others, do not be afraid to say what you have found and what you value. Appreciate that doubt and questioning can also lead to spiritual growth and to a greater awareness of the Light that is in us all.

6.   Do you work gladly with other religious groups in the pursuit of common goals? While remaining faithful to Quaker insights, try to enter imaginatively into the life and witness of other communities of faith, creating together the bonds of friendship.

7.   Be aware of the spirit of God at work in the ordinary activities and experience of your daily life. Spiritual learning continues throughout life, and often in unexpected ways. There is inspiration to be found all around us, in the natural

world, in the sciences and arts, in our work and friendships, in our sorrows as well as in our joys. Are you open to new light, from whatever source it may come? Do you approach new ideas with discernment?

8.   Worship is our response to an awareness of God. We can worship alone, but when we join with others in expectant waiting we may discover a deeper sense of God's presence. We seek a gathered stillness in our meetings for worship so that all may feel the power of God's love drawing us together and leading us.

9.   In worship we enter with reverence into communion with God and respond to the promptings of the Holy Spirit. Come to meeting for worship with heart and mind prepared. Yield yourself and all your outward concerns to God's guidance so that you may find 'the evil weakening in you and the good raised up'.

10. Come regularly to meeting for worship even when you are angry, depressed, tired and spiritually cold. In the silence ask for and accept the prayerful support of others joined with you in worship. Try to find a spiritual wholeness which encompasses suffering as well as thankfulness and joy. Prayer, springing from a deep place in the heart, may bring healing and unity as nothing else can. Let meeting for worship nourish your whole life.

11. Be honest with yourself. What unpalatable truths might you be evading? When you recognise your shortcomings, do

not let that discourage you. In worship together we can find the assurance of God's love and the strength to go on with renewed courage.

12. When you are preoccupied and distracted in meeting let wayward and disturbing thoughts give way quietly to your awareness of God's presence among us and in the world. Receive the vocal ministry of others in a tender and creative spirit. Reach for the meaning deep within it, recognising that even if it is not God's word for you, it may be so for others. Remember that we all share responsibility for the meeting for worship whether our ministry is in silence or through the spoken word.

13. Do not assume that vocal ministry is never to be your part. Faithfulness and sincerity in speaking, even very briefly, may open the way to fuller ministry from others. When prompted to speak, wait patiently to know that the leading and the time are right, but do not let a sense of your own unworthiness hold you back. Pray that your ministry may arise from deep experience, and trust that words will be given to you. Try to speak audibly and distinctly, and with sensitivity to the needs of others. Beware of speaking predictably or too often, and of making additions towards the end of a meeting when it was well left before.

14. Are your meetings for church affairs held in a spirit of worship and in dependence on the guidance of God? Remember that we do not seek a majority decision nor even consensus. As we wait patiently for divine guidance our expe-

rience is that the right way will open and we shall be led into
unity.

15. Do you take part as often as you can in meetings for
church affairs? Are you familiar enough with our church government to contribute to its disciplined process? Do you
consider difficult questions with an informed mind as well as a
generous and loving spirit? Are you prepared to let your
insights and personal wishes take their place alongside those of
others or be set aside as the meeting seeks the right way
forward? If you cannot attend, uphold the meeting prayerfully.

16. Do you welcome the diversity of culture, language and
expressions of faith in our yearly meeting and in the world
community of Friends? Seek to increase your understanding
and to gain from this rich heritage and wide range of spiritual
insights. Uphold your own and other yearly meetings in your
prayers.

17. Do you respect that of God in everyone though it may be
expressed in unfamiliar ways or be difficult to discern? Each
of us has a particular experience of God and each must find
the way to be true to it. When words are strange or disturbing to you, try to sense where they come from and what has
nourished the lives of others. Listen patiently and seek the
truth which other people's opinions may contain for you.
Avoid hurtful criticism and provocative language. Do not
allow the strength of your convictions to betray you into
making statements or allegations that are unfair or untrue.
Think it possible that you may be mistaken.

18. How can we make the meeting a community in which each person is accepted and nurtured, and strangers are welcome? Seek to know one another in the things which are eternal, bear the burden of each other's failings and pray for one another. As we enter with tender sympathy into the joys and sorrows of each other's lives, ready to give help and to receive it, our meeting can be a channel for God's love and forgiveness.

19. Rejoice in the presence of children and young people in your meeting and recognise the gifts they bring. Remember that the meeting as a whole shares a responsibility for every child in its care. Seek for them as for yourself a full development of God's gifts and the abundant life Jesus tells us can be ours. How do you share your deepest beliefs with them, while leaving them free to develop as the spirit of God may lead them? Do you invite them to share their insights with you? Are you ready both to learn from them and to accept your responsibilities towards them?

20. Do you give sufficient time to sharing with others in the meeting, both newcomers and long-time members, your understanding of worship, of service, and of commitment to the Society's witness? Do you give a right proportion of your money to support Quaker work?

21. Do you cherish your friendships, so that they grow in depth and understanding and mutual respect? In close relationships we may risk pain as well as finding joy. When experiencing great happiness or great hurt we may be more open to the working of the Spirit.

22. Respect the wide diversity among us in our lives and relationships. Refrain from making prejudiced judgements about the life journeys of others. Do you foster the spirit of mutual understanding and forgiveness which our discipleship asks of us? Remember that each one of us is unique, precious, a child of God.

23. Marriage has always been regarded by Friends as a religious commitment rather than a merely civil contract. Both partners should offer with God's help an intention to cherish one another for life. Remember that happiness depends on an understanding and steadfast love on both sides. In times of difficulty remind yourself of the value of prayer, of perseverance and of a sense of humour.

24. Children and young people need love and stability. Are we doing all we can to uphold and sustain parents and others who carry the responsibility for providing this care?

25. A long-term relationship brings tensions as well as fulfilment. If your relationship with your partner is under strain, seek help in understanding the other's point of view and in exploring your own feelings, which may be powerful and destructive. Consider the wishes and feelings of any children involved, and remember their enduring need for love and security. Seek God's guidance. If you undergo the distress of separation or divorce, try to maintain some compassionate communication so that arrangements can be made with the minimum of bitterness.

26. Do you recognise the needs and gifts of each member of your family and household, not forgetting your own? Try to make your home a place of loving friendship and enjoyment, where all who live or visit may find the peace and refreshment of God's presence.

27. Live adventurously. When choices arise, do you take the way that offers the fullest opportunity for the use of your gifts in the service of God and the community? Let your life speak. When decisions have to be made, are you ready to join with others in seeking clearness, asking for God's guidance and offering counsel to one another?

28. Every stage of our lives offers fresh opportunities. Responding to divine guidance, try to discern the right time to undertake or relinquish responsibilities without undue pride or guilt. Attend to what love requires of you, which may not be great busyness.

29. Approach old age with courage and hope. As far as possible, make arrangements for your care in good time, so that an undue burden does not fall on others. Although old age may bring increasing disability and loneliness, it can also bring serenity, detachment and wisdom. Pray that in your final years you may be enabled to find new ways of receiving and reflecting God's love.

30. Are you able to contemplate your death and the death of those closest to you? Accepting the fact of death, we are freed to live more fully. In bereavement, give yourself time

to grieve. When others mourn, let your love embrace them.

31. We are called to live 'in the virtue of that life and power that takes away the occasion of all wars'. Do you faithfully maintain our testimony that war and the preparation for war are inconsistent with the spirit of Christ? Search out whatever in your own way of life may contain the seeds of war. Stand firm in our testimony, even when others commit or prepare to commit acts of violence, yet always remember that they too are children of God.

32. Bring into God's light those emotions, attitudes and prejudices in yourself which lie at the root of destructive conflict, acknowledging your need for forgiveness and grace. In what ways are you involved in the work of reconciliation between individuals, groups and nations?

33. Are you alert to practices here and throughout the world which discriminate against people on the basis of who or what they are or because of their beliefs? Bear witness to the humanity of all people, including those who break society's conventions or its laws. Try to discern new growing points in social and economic life. Seek to understand the causes of injustice, social unrest and fear. Are you working to bring about a just and compassionate society which allows everyone to develop their capacities and fosters the desire to serve?

34. Remember your responsibilities as a citizen for the conduct of local, national, and international affairs. Do not

shrink from the time and effort your involvement may demand.

35. Respect the laws of the state but let your first loyalty be to God's purposes. If you feel impelled by strong conviction to break the law, search your conscience deeply. Ask your meeting for the prayerful support which will give you strength as a right way becomes clear.

36. Do you uphold those who are acting under concern, even if their way is not yours? Can you lay aside your own wishes and prejudices while seeking with others to find God's will for them?

37. Are you honest and truthful in all you say and do? Do you maintain strict integrity in business transactions and in your dealings with individuals and organisations? Do you use money and information entrusted to you with the discretion and responsibility? Taking oaths implies a double standard of truth; in choosing to affirm instead, be aware of the claim to integrity that you are making.

38. If pressure is brought upon you to lower your standard of integrity, are you prepared to resist it? Our responsibilities to God and our neighbour may involve us in taking unpopular stands. Do not let the desire to be sociable, or the fear of seeming peculiar, determine your decisions.

39. Consider which of the ways to happiness offered by society are truly fulfilling and which are potentially corrupt-

ing and destructive. Be discriminating when choosing means of entertainment and information. Resist the desire to acquire possessions or income through unethical investment, speculation or games of chance.

40. In view of the harm done by the use of alcohol, tobacco and other habit-forming drugs, consider whether you should limit your use of them or refrain from using them altogether. Remember that any use of alcohol or drugs may impair judgement and put both the user and others in danger.

41. Try to live simply. A simple lifestyle freely chosen is a source of strength. Do not be persuaded into buying what you do not need or cannot afford. Do you keep yourself informed about the effects your style of living is having on the global economy and environment?

42. We do not own the world, and its riches are not ours to dispose of at will. Show a loving consideration for all creatures, and seek to maintain the beauty and variety of the world. Work to ensure that our increasing power over nature is used responsibly, with reverence for life. Rejoice in the splendour of God's continuing creation.

Be patterns, be examples in all countries, places, islands,
nations, wherever you come, that your carriage and life
may preach among all sorts of people, and to them; then
you will come to walk cheerfully over the world,
answering that of God in every one.
(George Fox, 1656)

NOTES AND REFERENCES

———◆———

Notes and references

Quotations that appear with just a number in brackets, refer to that numbered section in *Advices and Queries*.

1. Tennyson, Lord Alfred; *The Higher Pantheism*.
2. Fox, George; *Journal*, J.L. Nickalls, ed.; London Yearly Meeting, 1952.
3. John, 1:9.
4. Fox, George; *Journal* (as no. 2 above).
5. Matar, N.I.; *Some Notes on George Fox and Islam*, 'Journal of the Friends Historical Society', Vol. 55, No. 8, 1989.
6. George Fox's letter to ministers, 1656; quoted in *Quaker Faith and Practice* (hereafter *QFP*), 19.32, Britain Yearly Meeting, 1997.
7. Cock, Luke; (1721), quoted in *QFP*, 20.22.
8. Vellacott, Jo; (1982), quoted in *QFP*, 20.05.
9. Matthew, 7:21.
10. Southall, John Edward; *The Power of Stillness* (c. 1900); reprinted in part in the leaflet 'Silence', Quaker Home Service, 1996.
11. Barclay, Robert; *Apology for the True Christian Divinity*; quoted in *QFP*, 19.21.

12. Howgill, Francis; 1663; quoted in *QFP*, 19.08.

13. Story, Thomas; (1691) quoted in *Christian Faith and Practice* (earlier ed of *QFP*), London Yearly Meeting, 1960.

14. Stephen, Caroline; *Quaker Strongholds*, 1890; quoted in *QFP*, 2.02.

15. Matthews, 6:33.

16. Lacout, Pierre; *God is Silence*, Quaker Home Service, 1993.

17. Matthew, 18:20.

18. Adapted from *Friendly Bible Study* by Joanne and Larry Spears, Friends General Conference, Philadelphia, 1998.

19. Ibid.

20. Cadbury, Henry J.; *George Fox's Book of Miracles*, Cambridge University Press, 1948. To be reprinted in 1999 by QUIP (Quakers Uniting In Publications). No other details currently available.

21. Postcard published by the Fellowship of Reconciliation, Nyack, New York.

22. Lawrence, Brother; *The Practice of the Presence of God*, Samata Books, Madras, India, 1987.

23. Traditional Zen story.

24. Fox, George; *Journal* (as no. 2 above) entry for 1651; quoted in *QFP*, 24.01

25. *A Declaration from the harmless and innocent people of God called Quakers, against all plotters and fighters in the world*, 1660; quoted in *QFP*, 24.04.

26. Pennington, Isaac; *Somewhat spoken to a weighty question, concerning the magistrate's protection of the innocent*, 1661; quoted in *QFP*, 24:21.

27. *Statement issued by Aotearaoa/New Zealand Yearly Meeting*, 1987; quoted in *QFP*, 24:10.

28. Naylor, James; 'His Last Testimony', 1660, in *A collection of sundry books, epistles and papers*, 1716; quoted in *QFP*, 19.12.

29. Matthew, 5:37.

30. Pinney, Rachel;*Creative Listening*, third revised edition 1981, published by the author.

31. Ibid.

32. *The Nature and Variety of Concern; the report of a working party*, 1986, published on behalf of Meeting for Sufferings of the Religious Society of Friends by Quaker Home Service.

33. Ibid.

34. Tennyson, Margot; *Friends and Other Faiths*, 1992, Quaker Home Service.

35. Burrough, Edward; 1662; quoted in *Beyond Majority Rule* by Michael J. Sheeran, Philadelphia Yearly meeting, 1983.

36. 'General Counsel on Church Affairs', *QFP*, 3.07.

37. 'Quaker Marriage Procedure', *QFP*, chapter 16.

38. Ibid.

39. Galatians 2:20.

40. Luke 12:32.

BIBLIOGRAPHY
AND
USEFUL ADDRESSES

BIBLIOGRAPHY

I have put the books into rough categories, but the nature of Quakerism means that most books cover all aspects in one way or another. Books marked '(o/p)' are out of print at the time of writing, but may be reprinted. The dates given are those of the most recent edition. Most public libraries can obtain Quaker books, and most Quaker Meetings have libraries from which books can be borrowed. There is also a library at Friends House, and the Quaker Bookshop carries new and second-hand Quaker books (see Useful Addresses.)

MAJOR SOURCES USED IN THIS BOOK

Quaker Faith and Practice; the book of Christian discipline of the Yearly Meeting of the Religious Society of Friends (Quakers) in Britain, Britain Yearly Meeting (BYM), 1995. A collection of quotations old and new covering all aspects of Quakerism today as practised in the UK. Other Yearly Meetings, particularly in the USA, have their own versions of *Faith and Practice*. *QFP* is available in cloth or paperback, and in a large print edition.

Advices and Queries, BYM, 1995. This is part of *QFP*, but is also available separately as a small booklet (see Appendix 1).

Bibliography

QUAKERISM TODAY

A Light that is Shining, Harvey Gillman, Quaker Home Service (QHS), 1997. The 'official' introduction to Quakers today, particularly in the UK.

Who do we think we are? Young Friends Commitment and Belonging, the 1998 Swarthmore Lecture given by Young Friends General Meeting, QHS, 1998.

WORSHIP, MEDITATION AND PRAYER

The Amazing Fact of Quaker Worship, George Gorman, QHS, 1993.

Testimony of Devotion, Thomas Kelly, Harper Collins, 1996.

Nourishing the Spiritual Life, Paul A. Lacey, QHS, 1995.

God is Silence, Pierre Lacout, QHS, 1993. A modern Quaker classic now available in a pocket-size edition.

What Kind of God, What Kind of Healing, Jim Pym, Friends Fellowship of Healing (FFH), 1990.

Dear Gift of Life, a man's encounter with death, Bradford Smith, Pendle Hill Pamphlet #142, Wallingford, Pa., 1978.

Meditation, the Inward Art, Bradford Smith, George Allen and Unwin, 1964 (o/p).

Friendly Bible Study, Joanne and Larry Spears, Friends General Conference, Philadelphia, 1998.

Mutual Irradiation; a Quaker view of ecumenism, Douglas Steere, Pendle Hill Pamphlet #175, Wallingford, Pa., 1971.

Jung and the Quaker Way, Jack Wallis, QHS, 1989.

TESTIMONIES AND CONCERNS

Peace is a Process, Sydney Bailey, QHS, 1995.

Peace in the Power and the Light, David Lonsdale, SJ., QHS, 1988.

Bibliography

The Peace Kit; everyday peacemaking for young people, John Lampen, QHS, 1992.

Testimony and Tradition; some aspects of Quaker spirituality, John Punshon, QHS, 1990.

Beyond Majority Rule: voteless decisions in the Religious Society of Friends, Michael J. Sheeran, SJ., Philadelphia Yearly Meeting, 1983.

Friends and Other Faiths, Margot Tennyson, QHS, 1992.

The Nature and Variety of Concern; the report of a working party, QHS, for Meeting for Sufferings, 1992.

HISTORICAL

Let Your Words be Few; symbolism of speaking and silence among seventeenth century Quakers, Richard Baumann, Cambridge University Press, 1983. Reprinted by QHS, 1998.

George Fox's Book of Miracles, edited with introduction and notes by Henry J. Cadbury. First published by Cambridge University Press, 1948. To be re-issued by QUIP (Quakers Uniting in Publications), 1999.

George Fox and the Healing Ministry, David Hodges, FFH, 1995.

Mystical Reformers of the 16th and 17th Centuries, Rufus Jones, Macmillan and Co, (o/p).

Studies in Mystical Religion, Rufus Jones, Macmillan and Co, (o/p).

Journal of George Fox, edited by John L. Nickalls. London Yearly Meeting, 1975. The most accessible edition, being based on manuscript sources, and edited by the former Librarian at Friends House, London.

A Reader's Companion to George Fox's Journal, Joseph

Pickvance, QHS, 1989. An invaluable guide to the language and culture of Fox's Journal, based on the Nickalls edition.

George Fox and the Quakers, Cecil W. Sharman, QHS, 1991.

No More but My Love; letters of George Fox, Quaker, selected and edited by Cecil W. Sharman, QHS, 1980.

Quakers in India, Marjorie Sykes, George Allen and Unwin, 1998, (o/p).

OTHER BOOKS REFERRED TO

Creative Listening, Rachel Pinney, third revised edition, published by the author, London, 1981 (o/p).

The Cloud of Unknowing, Anon, translated by Ira Progoff, Rider Books, 1959 (o/p).

The Practice of the Presence of God, Brother Lawrence. This book – as well as the preceding one – has been published many times by different publishers, and several editions may be in print. The edition I have used is published by Samata Books, Madras, India, and is distributed by the Ramakrishna Vedanta Centre, Bourne End, Bucks.

Zen Mind, Beginners Mind, Shunryu Suzuki, weatherill Publishers, New York and Tokyo.

Notes to Myself, Hugh Prather, Bantam Books, 1996.

USEFUL ADDRESSES

Central headquarters of Quakers in the UK:
  Britain Yearly Meeting
  Friends House
  Euston Road
  London NW1 2BJ
  Tel: 0171 663 1000
  Fax: 0171 663 1001
  WWW: http://www.quaker.org

The major departments which have been mentioned in this book, and are to be found at the above address are:

  The Library of the Religious Society of Friends.
  Quaker Home Service *(deals with meetings, the spiritual life of Friends, publishing and matters relating to children and young people. Contact them for information about Quakers, free literature and the address of your nearest local meeting.)*
  Quaker Peace and Service *(deals with matters relating to the peace witness, and overseas service.)*
  Quaker Bookshop *(new and second-hand books on Quakerism and allied subjects such as peace and social*

studies, the spiritual life, mysticism and comparative religion)

Quaker Social Responsibility and Education *(deals with matters relating to social responsibility in the UK, such as care of the elderly, homelessness etc, and with education.)*

For information about Quakers outside the UK:
Friends World Committee for Consultation
4 Byng Place
London WC1E 7JH
Tel: 0171 388 0497
Fax: 0171 383 4644

For information on Quakers in the USA (all traditions), contact:
Quaker Information Center
1501 Cherry Street
Philadelphia
Pa. 19102
USA
Tel: +215 241-7024

Accommodation in London, and conferences:
Quaker International Centre
1–3 Byng Place
London WC1E 7JH
Tel: 0171 387 5648
Fax: 0171 383 3722
For details of other accommodation, contact Friends House.

Useful Addresses

The Friends Fellowship of Healing also have accommodation, and details of this and their other activities can be obtained from:

Friends Fellowship of Healing
c/o Alan Pearce
20 Burnet Avenue
Burpham
Guildford
Surrey GU1 1YD
Tel: 01483 569257

For Quaker retreats etc:

Q-ROOM (Quaker Retreats and One-to-One Ministry)
c/o Linda Brasher
Zennor
Amherst Hill
Riverhead
Sevenoaks
Kent TN13 3DS

Charney Manor
Charney Bassett
Wantage
Oxfordshire OX12 0EJ
Tel: 01235 868206

Useful Addresses

For educational courses, and conferences contact:
Woodbrook College
1046 Bristol Road
Selly Oak
Birmingham B29 6LJ
Tel: 0121 472 5171
Fax: 0121 472 5173

For a study of the mystical aspects of Quakerism, through a magazine, postal discussion groups and conferences, contact:
The Seekers Association
c/o Judith Chandler
12 Vyvian Terrace
Bristol BS8 3DG

Other Quaker informal Groups include those listed below. Many of these publish their own literature and newsletters. Addresses can be obtained from Friends House.
Northern Friends Peace Board
Friends Historical Society
Young Friends General Meeting
Friends Vegetarian Society
Quaker Concern for
Animals
Quaker Fellowship of the Arts
Quaker Green Concern
Quaker Homeless Action
Quaker Lesbian and Gay Fellowship
Quaker Universalist Group
Quaker Women's Group